Learn
SMALL BUSINESS
START–UP in 7 DAYS

Learn
SMALL BUSINESS
START–UP in 7 DAYS

HEATHER SMITH

Wrightbooks

First published in 2013 by Wrightbooks
an imprint of John Wiley & Sons Australia, Ltd
42 McDougall St, Milton Qld 4064

Office also in Melbourne

Typeset in 11.3/14 pt ITC Berkeley Oldstyle Std

© Heather Nicolette Smith 2013

The moral rights of the author have been asserted

National Library of Australia Cataloguing-in-Publication data:

Author:	Smith, Heather (Heather Nicolette).
Title:	Learn small business start-up in 7 days: Launch a lean, efficient start-up / Heather Smith.
ISBN:	9780730378235 (pbk.)
Notes:	Includes index.
Subjects:	Learning.
	Small business.
	New business enterprises.
	Success in business.
Dewey Number:	658.022

Cover design by Xou Creative

MYOB® is a registered trademark of MYOB Technology Pty Ltd and its affiliates.

Printed in China by Printplus Limited

10 9 8 7 6 5 4 3 2 1

Disclaimer

Contents

About the author

In the 1940s Heather Smith's grandfather, Ashley Smith, wrote *A City Stirs*. He spent a day in London, observing activity from the crack of dawn until when the city went to sleep. Heather says, 'I write very much like my grandfather. I observe what happens with the businesses I consult into, and I write about it. People tell me that when I articulate something, it can set off a light bulb moment, and can help them in their own business. I know small businesses inside out and upside down, and my expertise combined with my education and experiences enable me to help small businesses. Through writing, speaking and consulting I aim to help as many small businesses as possible, and maximise their productivity and profitability.'

Heather utilises remote technology to connect with the businesses and is able to provide education, training and support across Australia. She writes for, and has been quoted in, national online and printed publications, including *Latte*, Flying Solo (a website for **solopreneurs**), My Business (a website for business advice), ninemsn, *Woman's Day*, *The Daily Telegraph*, the *Courier Mail*, the *Dynamic Business* website and *Network* magazine. She has a bachelor of commerce degree from Griffith University in Queensland and is a Management

Accountant, and a fellow and ambassador of the Association of Chartered Certified Accountants (ACCA). Heather is a **XERO** and **MYOB** consultant. Her first book was *Learn MYOB in 7 Days*, and she has started work on her third book, a guide to the cloud accounting solution XERO.

Heather has enthusiastically embraced the world of technology and social media, and uses both to help her connect with small-business people and to understand their most pressing issues. She is available for speaking engagements, workshops and online consultations.

Connect with Heather:

▶ Website: www.HeatherSmithSmallBusiness.com

▶ LinkedIn: www.linkedin.com/in/HeatherSmithAU

▶ Twitter: @HeatherSmithAU

▶ Facebook: www.facebook.com/HeatherSmithAU.

Acknowledgements

While cleaning out my cupboards I found a dusty book proposal from more than 10 years ago. I have always dreamed of being a published author but I never had the confidence to go through with the final submission. I am so grateful to Kristen Hammond, who watched my prolific ramblings about small business across social media channels, took me by the hand and mentored me through the whole process of writing a book. Thank you also to Elizabeth Whiley, Sandra Balonyi and all the team at Wiley.

This book would not have been possible without my clients. I am very thankful to all my clients, who have invited me into their businesses and provided me with the opportunity of working with them. We are living through an exciting evolution of the small business. Million-dollar, multinational microbusinesses can operate out of cosy home offices. Digital nomads outsource business operations while travelling the world and enjoying the experiences that life has to offer. People wanting flexibility can create a business selling their niche expertise. I am elated that I can be a part of this journey with so many businesses.

Thank you to Valerie Khoo (@ValerieKhoo) and the Sydney Writers' Centre community. Thank you, Valerie, for challenging me and believing in me. Special thanks to Alistair McKillop (@AliBali61), a SWC student and published author, who kindly provided feedback on the manuscript.

Thank you to Sam Leader, Robert Gerrish and the Flying Solo community for their never-faltering support.

Thank you to the many small business rock stars who educate, motivate and inspire me.

To my mum and dad, family and friends — thank you. To the best friends a girl could have, Bridget, Tania and Sharron — thank you. To my raison d'être, my children — everything in my world revolves around you, Christopher and Charlotte. Thank you for just being you and making me so proud every day. Thank you to Charlie. Every writer should have a dog like Charlie. He sits at my feet for endless hours and every so often drops a ball at my feet, knowing I need to take a break and encouraging me to get away from the desk and into the backyard for a play. Finally, muchas gracias to my husband, Simon. Words cannot express how grateful, how lucky and how fortunate I am to have you in my life: xxx.

Introduction

Congratulations on taking the first step on the exciting journey of starting your own business! Today is about you and assessing if you are ready to start a business. We are going to explore what is involved in running a business and evaluate if you have the discipline, skills, focus, enthusiasm, determination and energy to take your idea and turn it into a business.

I have worked with hundreds of business owners during the start-up phase of their business. I am here to share everything I have learned along the way from their successes and mistakes. I wrote this book with you in mind. I am writing as if I am talking with the many clients I have worked with, and sharing with you everything I have learned along the way.

I thought about starting a business for about 18 months before I actually launched my own consulting business. I read everything I could get my hands on, asked lots of questions and pondered the possibilities. I spent two weeks in Maleny—in a lovely, tranquil cottage on the top of a hill—focused on crafting a business plan. Then, finally, I launched my business ... and I have not looked back since.

Maybe you won't take as long to start a business, or maybe you will take longer. *Learn Small Business Start-Up in 7 Days* will take you step by step through all the aspects that you need to consider and plan for when starting your own business.

As you embark on the road of launching your own business, you will begin a process of learning, unlearning and relearning. I recall a discussion with a business owner who had worked for a 'big 4' accounting consulting firm and was paid extraordinarily well to tell people how to improve the operations of their own business. Then she took the leap of faith and started her own business, and was flabbergasted by how little she actually understood about running a business, and how much she learned during the first few years. The practical side of running a successful business unfortunately does not always follow the theoretical teachings of business school or books. You will be overwhelmed, yet hopefully stimulated and excited, at how much you will learn and experience in the early days of your own business.

This book is packed full of questions that you should contemplate. I am going to present you with questions and information that will help you make your decisions and plan your business's future. I am also going to share with you lots of stories along the way of what I have seen that has worked and what has not worked.

You will have to make decisions, but if at any time you realise you have not made the right decision, you can review your options and change your course of action. That's okay. It's part of the evolution of your small business. To start a successful business you need to do your homework and groundwork. And *you will have to develop a plan*. Without a plan a business cannot be successful, so don't kid yourself that you can skip this step. You then need to implement your plan.

The purpose of this book is to empower you with the knowledge and understanding for starting a business. Each chapter of the book discusses one area of business start-up. Altogether there are seven main areas and ideally you should put aside one day for each of these.

On day 1 we will explore the question, 'Are you ready to start a business?' Then, on day 2, we will review the steps required to establish your business.

Part of commencing a business involves seeking professional advice. On day 3 we will discuss the professional advice you will need and where you can go to find it.

Day 4 is dedicated to teaching you how to market your business. Some business theorists believe marketing is the most important aspect of a business. What do you need to know about marketing and how can you effectively use marketing to promote your own business?

On day 5 we will focus on my favourite topic, finances: the tax obligations you need to be aware of, record keeping, and which reports you should be generating and using to assist you in managing your business.

Following a day of finances, we will spend day 6 exploring your business's most important asset — and most likely your greatest expense — your employees. Will you employ staff? How will you hire and train them? What procedures and processes do you have in place for staff to follow?

Finally, on day 7, with a foundation of knowledge and understanding in place, we will go through the steps involved in launching your business.

Some people have the mindset that starting a business means getting a big loan; maxing out credit cards; spending lots of money; investing in the best whiz-bang offices, websites and people; and following the philosophy 'build it and they will come'. They think that by throwing money at their business, customers will magically appear. Unfortunately, real life does not mimic the movies.

I will unabashedly encourage you to launch your business as leanly as possible: bootstrap the business, invest your own funds in the business, live frugally and watch every penny you spend. The less money you spend, the less profit you need to generate to turn your business into a success. The less money you borrow, the more control you have over the business. Once the business is profitable and returning a positive cash flow, you are then in a position to distribute funds to yourself and reap the rewards of your success.

Long-term successful businesses are not the ones with the most money spent on them, or with the smartest owner (or with the owner who works the longest hours); they are the ones where the leader consistently makes the right decisions for the business. As founder of the business, this is what your role will be: making the right decisions.

How do you make the correct decision in a timely manner? Personally I gather the available data, information, feedback and options and assess these against the **ROI**. What is ROI? **Return on Investment**. What will the return be to the business for the investment made? The investment is typically in the form of money, although it may also take the form of time. A time investment may be referred to as engagement: **ROE**, or **Return on Engagement**. The return may encompass a broad spectrum of concepts (productivity, exposure, community involvement, sustainability and so on), but essentially the return needs to be assessed as a dollar figure. I am not saying that for every business decision a business needs to be profitable. What I am saying is that the business needs to clearly understand what will be the dollar outcomes of the decision. For example, if a business decides to employ an additional staff member, what effect will that have on profit? If a business decides to invest in an advertising campaign, what effect will that have on profit? If a business decides to reduce its health and safety budget, what are the potential effects on profit? Likewise, if an accident occurs and you are deemed to be negligent, how will this affect your profit? Return on Investment is an important concept that needs to be understood and applied to the decisions as you work your way through developing your own business.

You will be amazed at how many microdecisions you will have to make when starting a business, and some of them will not excite you at all, but they will still have to be made—and usually very quickly. If the business is opening in an established industry, there should be resources and mentors available; that is, successful businesses that you can learn from. If, however, you are bringing an innovative, never-before-seen business to market, making decisions may be really hard. There will be no informed resource that you can turn to, and instead you may have to rely on your gut instincts and monitor the option chosen.

I have designed this book to be read in chapter order, as it works through the typical timeline and processes involved in starting a business. I suggest you read through the chapters, and then come back to any particular section should you need to review a particular area.

Day 1

Are you ready to start a business?

Key areas we will cover on day 1:

▶ defining 'small business'

▶ setting goals for a business

▶ managing a work-life balance

▶ choosing a business idea

▶ undertaking market research

▶ understanding the competition and business environment

▶ avoiding the pitfalls of starting a business.

What is a small business?

How do you define a small business? Interestingly, there seems to be no universal definition. Various government authorities have suggested definitions that centre around ownership, turnover and assets. I think it comes down to simply the number of people employed within the business. Yes—just this one, simple measurement. I think one to four people represents a microbusiness, and five to 20 represents a small business. In today's internet age, multimillion-dollar businesses can be run by a couple from their garage. It seems odd to suggest they are anything other than a microbusiness.

Goals for running a business

Have you determined what your personal goals are for running a business? What are your objectives for running a business? What are you hoping to achieve? Have you set yourself a time frame?

A common business methodology for formulating goals is to apply the **SMART goal** framework (first mentioned by George T. Doran in *Management Review*, November 1981): specific, measurable, attainable, relevant and timely. The SMART criterion is used to formulate a goal with substance. So, rather than suggesting your goal is:

'I want to start a business and make lots of money'

you would say:

'Within six months I want to start a home-based business that will sell Australian-made body lotions all over the world and generate a regular income of $4000 per month so that I will have more time to spend with my family'.

The latter goal can be broken down and matched with the SMART goal framework:

▶ *Specific.* The specific goal is to 'start a home-based business that will sell Australian-made body lotions all over the world', indicating what the goal setter wants to achieve.

▶ *Measurable.* The measurable goal is to achieve a dollar figure income per month, which in this case is to 'generate a regular income of $4000 per month'.

▶ *Attainable.* With the right resources it seems like an achievable and realistic goal. If the time frame had been shorter — say, six weeks — or if the regular income had been higher — for example, $10 000 — the goal, while potentially achievable, would seem unattainable.

▶ *Relevant.* 'More time to spend with my family' gives some meaning and purpose to the goal. Essentially the goal setter hopes the business will not take up too much time.

▶ *Timely.* The timely goal is 'within six months', indicating by when the goal setter hopes to achieve the goal.

What are your goals for starting a business? You may see a gap in the market and believe you could start a business to address that need. You may have a hobby and want to see if it has commercial potential. You may want to start a business to get away from something. Maybe you are simply fed up with laughing at your boss's jokes, corporate culture, or working in a business that operates inefficiently and you think you can do it better yourself.

If you are fed up with reporting to a boss and want to start a business so you no longer have to report to anyone, think again. A business owner reports to customers, to the bank, to the tax office and other government departments — to anyone with a vested interest in the business. There is a line of people you will have to answer to. Once you are running your own business, you may find that you actually have more appreciation for the job that your boss did. Running a business has many rewards, but it is not always the easy option.

Individuals have various reasons for starting a business. It may be to make money or to create a work-life balance around their family. An inventor may see it as a way of bringing an innovative product to the market. You may have been made unemployed, and due to a lack of suitable jobs, may see it as a way of creating a job for yourself. You may see it as a way of helping people and sharing knowledge efficiently. You may be frustrated with the current personal taxation system and want to take advantage of the tax benefits of running a business. Are your reasons for starting a business valid?

Activity 1.1

What are your personal SMART goals for running a business? Remember to address specific, measurable, attainable, realistic and timely goal criteria.

Are you suited to running a business?

You need self-motivation, determination, drive, resilience and knowledge to run a business. Once you have started a business, you may find the business environment is not as you predicted it to be, and you may need to exploit different opportunities. Your goals may change and evolve, but you need to start with goals and plans.

On day 2 we will start developing a business plan. Understanding your business goals will assist you in formulating a solid business plan. You will also need to make decisions about everything to do with your business. Personally I find that I am constantly faced with working through so many decisions in my business that when it comes to personal decisions I am totally spent! I don't care if you give me tea, coffee, macchiato or a skinny latte—as long as it's hot, I'm okay with it!

Are you suited to starting and running a business? Will you stay focused and motivated? Are you decisive? Are you faced with trepidation or excitement at the prospect of running your own business?

Part of the process of contemplating starting a business must involve assessing whether you and your personality traits are suited to running a business. You may have a great product and a captive market, but the long-term success of the business will depend on your ability to launch, manage and grow the business.

I once trained a female business owner in the basics of MYOB accounting software. Her business quickly developed into an award-winning, nationally successful business. While she did not spend time entering transactional data for her business, the MYOB training helped her source financial information within the MYOB accounting software and she used the information to assist her in making informed decisions. Would you benefit from additional training and knowledge before starting your business?

Do you want to be the boss? Are you comfortable that you will need to make a lot of decisions and be responsible for those decisions? Certainly you may employ staff and delegate roles and decisions to them, but ultimately the responsibility and risk remains with you. You may reap the rewards, but you may also lose your investment capital if the business does not go as expected. Running a business can be stressful. Do you want the responsibility and the stress that comes with it?

Do you have the time commitment to run a business? Speak to any successful business owner and they will tell you they spend a lot of time in their business. A business does not just stop at 5 pm on a Friday afternoon. Businesses are not predictable. Staff members may call in sick at short notice, and suddenly you find yourself working yet another shift in the business, rather than leading the business.

Are you prepared to give up evenings, weekends and holidays for your business? Are the people around you prepared for this? Do you have the energy for this?

Are you focused and self-disciplined and do you have a strong belief in yourself? Can you remain motivated to run your own business? Can you stay focused on one project, or do you easily get distracted and develop new passions every week? Do you think you have the commitment required to launch a business? Do you have a belief in yourself that will carry you through the difficult periods and help you make the hard decisions? I have a talented and hard-working friend who works long hours in the retail industry. She has talked about starting her own business for years, but has never taken the leap of faith. Rather than investing in her own development and taking charge of her life, she spends her time doing overtime for an unappreciative boss about whom she complains all the time. Her job totally depresses her. However, she has a mortgage and is worried about how she will pay it off in the long term if she leaves the security of employment. I don't know if starting her own business will turn her life around, but I hate seeing her so depressed and lacking belief in herself.

Do you have the knowledge, experience, industry know-how and skills to run a business? When people invest in your business or do business with you, they will be keen to know the prior experience you are bringing to the venture. A small business owner needs to wear many different hats and coordinate many different priorities while juggling a work-life balance. Running a business full time involves passion, 24/7 dedication and a huge commitment.

Don't get me wrong, starting a small business has many benefits, but there are always aspects that you may not like or that you may have little understanding of. Yet the responsibility for things like health and safety issues, chasing debts, deciding on marketing strategies, managing staffing rosters, choosing attractive colours for logos, and dealing with unreasonable customers fall squarely on your shoulders. These sorts of issues combined with long working hours and the isolation of being in charge must be considered. Can you cope with that responsibility? Do you know how to deal with all aspects of the business?

A local carpenter was working with a building company while planning to start his own business. He analysed where his experience gaps were, and undertook evening studies to complete his Building Services Authority licence, which was necessary for his own business start-up. He also arranged for his wife to undertake MYOB accounting software training so she could do the books for the business. When the carpenter eventually started his own business he would bring to the business relevant skills, experience and certifications.

As you read through this book you may identify areas that you need to spend more time understanding. Of course, you don't need to know every aspect of the operations. There are consultants and qualified staff available to shoulder some areas, and there is a vast wealth of knowledge available for free online at the 'Google University'. If you launch an airline no-one expects you to fly the planes.

Before you start a business you should assess whether there are gaps in your knowledge. Would you benefit from spending some time learning about a certain area? Can you develop your knowledge through a business course or work experience, either in your current role or in a new contract position or even a voluntary position?

Activity 1.2

- What personality traits do you have that are suited to starting a business?

- Are there gaps in your knowledge? Would you benefit from additional training?

- What relevant experience do you bring to the business?

Work-life balance

Business commitment can take many shapes and forms, and I don't want to scare you off with thoughts of never having a holiday again! You will, however, have to become very skilled at managing your time productively. There are only 24 hours in a day, and try as you may, you cannot change that. Your work, your health, your family and your life rely on your ability to be productive.

You only need to look at BRW's annual rich lists to see that there are some very unhealthy and overweight successful business people—over the long term this is not desirable. So think about how can you integrate an acceptable work-life balance into your business from the outset.

Clearly understanding the goals of your business and what you want to achieve with your business will assist in planning the structure of your daily business life. You may want to start a business on the side, or a home-based business, for some extra income simply so you can have a flexible lifestyle while generating some income. There are a growing number of **mumpreneurs**, **dadpreneurs** and **greypreneurs** who run small, successful businesses around family or retirement commitments. They may opt to forsake growing the business and employing staff, and the inevitable stress, by establishing a small, home-based business, working during school hours or working when the bowls tournaments are not on!

On the other hand, you may be ready to launch an empire and live and breathe your business 80 hours a week.

You need to establish daily exercise and healthy eating routines and incorporate them into your day. Can you ride to the workplace or swap business lunches for meetings on the squash court? I sign up for charity fun runs, get involved in community events, and publicise what I am doing through social media and my newsletter, combining my efforts with promoting my business. You will need to establish workplace boundaries and a planned daily schedule.

Where will your business be located? If your business starts at home, do you have dedicated space and dedicated time when the family will not disturb you? If the location of your business is outside of the home, how long does it take to get to your business location? Are you using your travel time productively? Would you benefit from investing in a chauffeur and a laptop for long trips?

My own business started on the kitchen table while children watched TV in the lounge room. Once I was more established, I took over a dedicated room in the house, and my turnover seemed to take a significant leap with this move! Most of the work I now do is **in the clouds** (internet based) and I operate as a digital nomad. I can work from anywhere I can connect to the internet.

Another person I know works in the import/export business. Initially they started the business at home. This was good for the cash flow while the business established itself. However, more and more parcels were being sent to the house until eventually the front foyer was filled with boxes and you had to jump over them every time you visited. The importer/exporter looked around for suitable offices and eventually found another import/export business conveniently located close to the airport that could rent them a large room. This was a great location for the growing business as the owners were able to undertake their business while receiving goods into the warehouse, enabling them to separate their business from their work life. If the business grows further one day they may look at expanding their office facilities.

For your own sanity you need to maintain some structure to your day. When do you work best? What do you need to keep your business mojo in top form? Perhaps driving your kids to school, or a boxing session two afternoons a week clears your head and gets you in the mood for work. Current thoughts around productivity are that multitasking is a myth and less is more. To be effective, understand when you are most productive and target those hours of the day by removing all distractions and focusing on work.

As a mother juggling school kids, I would get up early and work for an hour before they woke up, then get them ready and take them to school, before returning to do a solid five hours' work before pick-up time. After dinner I would settle down to my third session of work from 8 pm until late. I was working long hours, and had no 'me' time, which was unhealthy and eventually I realised it was also unproductive. I now avoid working late, ensure I get at least seven hours of sleep, and when I do get up early I arrange to go for a jog with my dog Charlie and a friend.

If you are suited to running a business and you launch a business suited to you, you will not have to wrestle with a work-life balance. You will simply be living.

Activity 1.3

- How will you structure your work day?
- How will you incorporate daily exercise into your routine?

Finding a product or service to sell

What products or services will your business sell? If you don't know what business you want to start, but have a burning desire to start something, there are a number of avenues you can look to for inspiration. I suggest you get yourself a blank book from the local stationery store and write in it anything that interests you: words, pictures, drawings, stories, cut-outs—anything at all. Over time you may see a pattern of what you are passionate about, and from that realisation consider whether you can turn your passion into profit.

Fortunately today, with the vast wealth of ideas available freely on the internet, the easiest way to generate business ideas is to simply do a search of 'top businesses to start in 20XX' or 'profitable businesses to start'. Each search returns more than 50 000 links to further inspiration and information. A site called www.springwise.com has a plethora of ideas. Springwise is an ideas database for entrepreneurs that categorises business ideas by industry. Offline you could contact your local government offices, such as Business Enterprise Centre (BEC), or find out if there are business or franchising expos where you can learn more about business opportunities.

Be careful before you hand over any money to schemes like 'I will show you how you can make money staying at home' signs pinned to telegraph poles. I suspect they are making most of their money by selling those schemes.

I know I spent more than a year working out what sort of business I should go into. There is a plethora of options: leaving a job and starting a similar business, starting your own business, buying a business, buying into a **franchise** or starting your own franchise. The number of choices can become overwhelming. Gather knowledge, listen and talk to people, and attend expos. Many people who launch a business may end up consulting back to their previous employees. These clients can initially be your bread and butter while your business establishes itself. Don't be too proud to work for them, and never burn bridges!

Activity 1.4

What products or services will your business sell?

Does your business idea have merit?

How do you assess whether your business idea has merit? How do you ascertain if your business idea will have receptive customers open to your offerings to ensure your business model is profitable?

Depending on the size of the business that you are planning to start, you could establish an advisory group to discuss, investigate and explore the business concept. You could access online business **forums** and discuss your business concept with other forum members. An active business forum to visit is www.flyingsolo.com.au. You could also talk to existing business owners within a similar industry and discuss the concepts and viability with colleagues.

As you explore the practicality of your business idea, you may be wondering whether you should keep it a secret. Will someone steal your business idea? A stealthy start-up involves keeping your idea to yourself until the launch. The downside of a stealthy start-up is that you will not get the feedback you need to react quickly to what users think of your product. Don't build past what you need to build to start getting feedback. I have come across people who are very secretive about what they do and they ask me to sign a non-disclosure statement. I actually consult to businesses on a regular basis not having any idea what they really do! Yes, I agree that some aspects of your business should be kept secret to maintain a competitive advantage, but your business idea may benefit from being critiqued by other people.

To assess the merit of your business idea you need to undertake market research, understand the regions, understand the culture, understand how the product or service fits in the market place, review potential competition within the industry, understand the business environment and prepare a forecast budget. If you are concerned about who you should invite into your inner business circle, do your **due diligence**. Then, if you feel it is necessary, get them to sign a non-disclosure statement.

Activity 1.5

- Does your business idea have merit?

- Is there a demand for the products or services you plan to sell?

Researching your business idea

Market research is a process of understanding, exploring and defining the market your business intends to operate in. It is about understanding and profiling your customers. Where are they located? What is their average age? What is their income bracket? What do they need? What do they want?

It is tempting to avoid or neglect undertaking market research and to assume that everyone thinks like you or that you clearly understand the market you plan to sell to. But *assuming* makes an *ass* out of *you* and *me*! Rather than launch the business on gut instinct it is prudent to take the time to understand the market and make informed strategic decisions about your business. Market research can be undertaken to gather information about customers or the market the business will operate in. Market research is used to discover what people want, need, believe or even the way they will act. Market research will profile potential clients and the best way to access them. It may include feasibility and benchmark studies; customer satisfaction surveys; and client, competitor and industry profiles. In reality your market research budget should probably directly correlate with how many resources you intend to invest in this venture.

So, who do you go to for market research? There are businesses that specialise in undertaking market research and if your business is a high-value commitment, you would be prudent to invest in paid market research.

Alternatively, you can undertake market research yourself. If you're working on a shoestring budget, there are a number of low-cost market research routes you can follow. The Australian Bureau of Statistics (ABS) has key statistical data available about the economy, people, different industries and regional statistics on its website at www.abs.gov.au. If you're reading this outside of Australia, your own government is likely to have a similar resource. I have visited the ABS website a number of times and it has some really interesting data. However, if you are new to the website, you may need to contact them for guidance in navigating their website.

For a minimal outlay you can post an advertisement on Facebook or LinkedIn, or use Google AdWords to promote your 'proposed' business products or services before they are available to establish if they generate interest from the buying public. This exercise works particularly well for internet businesses. If you wanted to take it a step further you could develop a landing page to collect potential leads and then contact them once the business is launched.

There are also online survey sites that enable you to create and distribute a questionnaire and analyse the results. I have used Survey Monkey www.surveymonkey.com, which is free but also has enhanced paid products. These websites all have a similar set-up: you craft questions, forward questions to potential respondents and then analyse the online results. They are a quick way of assessing whether you are making the right decisions, and a way of building a community around your venture. Many of those surveyed may feel a sense of connection with the business and be invested in its success. Obviously, it is good to have potential customers awaiting the launch of your business!

Activity 1.6

- What profile do you have of the business's ideal customer?

- What market research can you do to assess the viability of your business concept?

Understanding your competition

Do you have a clear idea who your competition will be? Do you know how to find your competition? You could look locally to see who is situated in the area, or use search engines, the yellow pages, or the local newspaper to discover who your competition may be.

Have you eaten in their restaurant, tried their services and bought their products? Are their clients loyal or price driven? Do you understand what your competition's strengths are and what you will be able to do differently?

A dietitian was growing her own practice and wanted to know and understand what were the best tools and techniques she should implement in her business. So she visited other dietitians, as a patient, to really understand what the experience was like and what worked and what didn't. She visited numerous other dietitians across the world from big, bustling cities to quiet regional towns, and took the best aspects of their practices and implemented them in her own.

Her research into her competitors was quite a costly yet informative exercise and, yes, she has a very successful practice.

Before I launched a business, I created a new email address and emailed my potential competition with a general small-business query to gather data, to see how they responded and to understand what they were charging. The responses were interesting. Some had a very professional standard response, some refused to respond to my question and would only deal with me via phone, and others responded and sent numerous follow-up responses (and then I found I was signed up to their newsletter). One lady sent me a huge email about troubles with her washing and how this delayed her response, and finally asked how she could help. For me it was interesting to see how so few of the responses actually answered my direct questions, and how they neglected to follow up with me.

Now that I am well entrenched in my own business, I don't see competition as the enemy. I see them as colleagues, as a resource, as a back-up plan when I am over-committed and as support. As a business owner I regularly communicate with many people who, on the outside, could be perceived to be my competition. Of course there are those I tend to avoid — those I do not refer work to and I do not speak about — but, in general, if I have a business problem the first person I typically call is a fellow business owner.

Activity 1.7

- Do you understand what competitive advantages and disadvantages your business has? Why are you better than your competitors?

Competitor	Overview	What are their strengths/ weaknesses	What are their prices? How do your products compare?	How will your business be better than your competitors'?

- Why will your customers or clients prefer to purchase products or services from your business rather than from your competitors?

Understanding the business environment

There is never a right time to start a business. Serendipity, luck and riding the crest of a trend wave can play a part in your business success. As you contemplate starting a business you need to look at the current business cycle. The business cycle refers to periods of expansion and contraction, which generally consist of four phases—recession, recovery, boom and contraction. It is difficult to predict the movement of the business cycle as each phase may be different in length and intensity. Will the economic environment be receptive to your new venture or are there barriers that you need to be aware of?

Evaluating the business environment

As I write this book, the Australian economy is confused. We are going through a mining boom, which is putting pressure on interest rates to go up; however, smaller businesses are finding the economy tight. People are saving rather than spending and retailers are seeing a decline in sales. With a strong Australian dollar, people are buying from online retailers based overseas. We went through a phase of chain stores opening everywhere. Then, after the al-Qaeda attack on the United States on 11 September 2001 a trend emerged to buy locally. Farmers' markets popped up and online retailers such as Etsy (www.etsy.com) and Madeit (www.madeit.com.au) emerged, selling homemade crafts globally.

Chain stores are shutting down and the number of small businesses is increasing. Perhaps for lifestyle choices and taxation reasons there is a growing number of solopreneurs leaving the corporate life and starting their own business. The government's reaction to this has been to review the taxation rules for 'consultants' and increase the red tape around typical sole-operated businesses. For example, bookkeepers who process business activity statements (BAS) now need to register as BAS agents with the Tax Practitioners Board (TPB) and adhere to various educational and insurance stipulations, which in turn has made operating more difficult and expensive.

The business environment is affected by taxation changes, government legislation and political changes. Although business owners have very little control over the business environment, they nevertheless need to be aware of it.

To stay in a successful business they may need to adapt and react to changes that take place. For example, if the government was reviewing the regulations regarding bike helmets, it would be unwise to pre-order a batch of bike helmets that only met current regulations as they may become obsolete before you have the opportunity to even bring them to market.

As a business owner you need to keep abreast of the business environment by listening to the business news. A favourite of mine is downloading Ross Greenwood's podcasts from his *Money News* radio program. Ross Greenwood is easy to understand and covers a wide range of business topics. You should also gather information from your industry bodies. For example, if you are planning to start a plumbing business, you would join an organisation such as the Master Plumbers and Mechanical Services Association of Australia and read the journals and newsletters they publish.

Activity 1.8

- Do you see any trends within your industry and will your business be able to take advantage of them?

- Describe the current market environment (refer to current population levels, employee availability, the economy and recent trends). Where will your business fit in this environment?

Avoiding mistakes

Through consulting, I come in contact with a lot of start-up microbusinesses and have discovered some of the mistakes they make. It is a driving force behind writing this book to share with you the many learnings that I have gathered along the way.

Sometimes the mistakes are small, simple and easily rectifiable. Sometimes they are costly, time consuming and, with some forethought, could have been avoided. Don't laugh—you'll be amazed at some of the mistakes as you read about them and you'll think, 'How could a sane business owner possibly make such a mistake?' Then you could find yourself several months down the track reflecting on this book and realising, 'Oops! I shouldn't be doing this!'

Expert advice

One of the problems I see facing new small business owners is that they don't seek expert advice. It can be beneficial to talk to friends and colleagues about your business venture, but you should not base your decisions on advice you heard at a pub. You should seek out unprejudiced specialists and professionals, listen to what they have to say and act upon their advice. Yes, you may well be paying for this advice, but it is likely to save you money in the long term. On day 3 we will explore the specialist and professional advice you as a business owner should be seeking.

Advertising

As you launch your business, understand what your capacity is and don't over-advertise. How many people can you serve? Don't promote or advertise your business beyond your capacity to serve your new clients.

One guy I heard about started a lawn mowing business and paid for 15 000 flyers to be distributed in his local area. When people called about his services, his father responded that his son had been inundated with enquiries and did not have time to mow their lawns.

Likewise, don't get publicity on a local current affairs news program only to find the overwhelming response crashes your website servers and disappoints potential customers.

Mates rates

One of the mistakes many businesses make in the start-up phase is providing discounted or free services to friends, family and charities. There are both good and bad reasons for doing this. You may appreciate the work experience and the opportunity to learn the ropes on a real-life customer or you may want to contribute to the community. However, by discounting your services you are lowering the value they perceive of the product or service your business is offering. When you use discounting to sell products you are just training your customers to wait for a sale and you may build this culture into your customers.

If you do want to offer a discount, I suggest you still invoice at full price and then detail the discount on the invoice so the customer is very clear of the value they are getting. I would also suggest you seek ways of leveraging off the discount you have offered to such customers: ask for advertising space in their charity newsletter, ask for referrals to potential paying clients, ask them to agree to be case studies, or ask them to write you a reference on LinkedIn to promote your services or products.

Start your business as you wish to continue. Beware of providing discounted services that eat into time you could be spending working fully billable hours or hours you could be using constructively finding billable work.

In our local community we have a well-networked business leader who expects businesses to provide her business with free services. She is very demanding and ungrateful, and if you don't service her she spreads negative vibes through her network. A number of us have been stung by her. It is really a tricky situation to extract your business from, and it would have been easier not to get into that situation at all! Just because you now own the business does not mean you have to offer your friends, family or charities freebies. Choose the pro bono work you want to do, and be firm with other requests.

Branded stationery

I cannot believe this topic is getting its own paragraph, but I see this mistake all the time, so it is worth mentioning. Don't invest in expensive branded stationery and then change the business name, structure or contact details so the stationery has to be thrown away. Do you really need branded stationery, or are you replicating big corporate business? If you do need stationery, can you purchase it in small batches or simply have the business logo developed and print it out as you need it?

Paths of communication

Decide how you want potential customers to contact the business. My advice would be not to give them too many options and to have it funnel in through a restricted number of avenues, otherwise you will be held hostage to numerous communication devices. Do you really want businesses to call your home number on the weekend?

Establish your business contact details and avoid having incorrect contact details on anything! Make sure you promote contact details on everything including your website and check that everything is correct—from the email signature to website listings. Also check that the business spam filter is not treating potential customers' emails as junk. Try contacting your business from an external source. What is the email or telephone response? Does it suit your business needs?

GST registration

Don't automatically register for the GST if you don't need to. Assess whether it is economically necessary to register for the GST and all the paperwork that comes with it. Also, don't issue tax invoices if you are not registered for the GST. The GST confuses a lot of people. (We will cover this issue in more depth on day 5.)

Self-discipline

Self-discipline is an important factor in avoiding mistakes so I would like to remind you to keep in mind these two points in particular: *stay focused* and *stay lean*.

While it's nice to focus on the parts of the business that you enjoy and understand, make sure you don't neglect the parts that don't interest you. You are responsible for everything now, so stay focused on all aspects of your business!

Don't overspend in the start-up phase. Yes, I am harping on it again and again — because business owners always tell me they wish they had not overspent in the beginning.

I don't believe any successful business has not made a mistake along the way. Hopefully this book can empower you to avoid them. A robust business will recognise an issue, deal with it and move on as part of its growth journey.

Getting additional help

There are many government and non-government resources available to assist you in starting your business.

▶ *NEIS*. The government currently funds a program for eligible job seekers who are interested in starting and running a small business called the **New Enterprise Incentive Scheme (NEIS).** As I write, the NEIS scheme can provide you with accredited small business training, business advice and mentoring, as well as ongoing income support for up to 52 weeks. I have worked with several small business owners who started on the NEIS scheme and have launched very successful businesses. Visit www.deewr.gov.au/Employment/JSA/EmploymentServices/Pages/NEIS.aspx.

▶ *BEC*. The Business Enterprise Centre (BEC) provides nationwide business advice and support to small and micro businesses. They offer business resources, how-to guides, seminars, forums and information on financing. Visit www.becaustralia.org.au.

▶ *TAFE*. TAFEs around Australia offer certificates in various courses such as Micro-Business Operations and Small Business Management that may fill in the gaps of your knowledge.

▶ *Libraries*. Local libraries have a vast collection of business books available for loan. Reservations can be placed online and books can be sourced from other libraries. I am a huge fan of the library and our local Brisbane City Council Library has even sourced books from interstate that I wanted to read. You can also borrow audio books via download and install them on your iPod, which is just amazing. I don't know whether your local library offers these services, but I encourage you to take the time to explore what they have on offer.

▶ *Banks.* Today many banks have a dedicated small business consultant who will meet with you and discuss your business's needs. The banks may also offer you literature, in-house courses and online forums that you can access. Of course they also have information on banking, credit facilities and merchant facilities that you may need to explore.

▶ *Industry groups.* Your own industry group may have resources to support you when starting a business such as information courses, networking and mentoring opportunities. For example, the Australian Institute of Professional Photography (AIPP) has a mentorship program for emerging members to assist photographers in their professional career. Maybe your industry association offers similar support.

▶ *Google University.* Okay, I really mean the internet. Search and you can find information about almost anything. Not everything on the internet is reliable, but a lot of people upload training videos, update Wikipedia—a free, web-based, collaborative, multilingual online encyclopedia project where contributors blog—and generally share their knowledge and insights.

▶ *Online business forums.* A forum is an online message board where people can discuss ideas related to a particular topic. There are a number of business-related websites that have a forum area you can access to discuss small-business issues. Some charge a membership fee and some are free. You can join anonymously or join and promote your business.

▶ *Business innovation centres or incubators.* A business **incubator** or innovation centre can be attached to a government-run or privately funded learning institute. It can be a location with shared offices for start-up and emerging businesses and it offers advice, support and mentoring to the business.

Activity 1.9

- Contact your local library and place a reservation on some business books. You can do this online.

- Contact your industry group. Do they offer support for start-up businesses?

Summary of day 1

The purpose of day 1 is for you to answer the question, 'Are you ready to start a business?' So, how do you feel? Do you think you are suited to running a business? If you are ready, go on with gusto! If you are feeling hesitant about starting a business, do you understand why?

I once met a young man who came into a nice inheritance. He bought into a business that he perceived would run itself. Unfortunately he appeared to have no interest in actually running a business. He seemed to have the notion that he would lead a hands-off, flexible lifestyle by owning a business, and his inheritance dwindled away. The experience was a costly business lesson for him. On the other hand I have met numerous older people—I call them greypreneurs—who say to me, 'Heather, I love my life and my business. I wish I had started my own business years ago!' I wonder if—had they indeed started their own business years ago, giving up the security of a job, superannuation and free access to a stationery cupboard—they would have been so content. We will never know.

If you don't feel ready to start your own business, can you overcome these barriers? If so, write down what you need to do so that you feel ready to start your own business, and include a time frame for each task. Overnight business success usually takes many years of hard work, so don't be dissuaded because you don't feel ready right now. Feel positive. You will either know a business owner's life is not for you, or you will have a blueprint of what you need to do to be ready to start a business.

Day 1 should have given you both a personal reflection and an appreciation of the business and business environment you are considering launching into. Don't allow yourself to drown in analysis paralysis, or allow a desire for perfection to stop you launching a business. With planning, support, knowledge and resources, owning your own business is possible and can be a part of your future.

On day 2 we will look at establishing the business and evolving your idea into a business structure. As you move through the week more of the pieces of this jigsaw will fall into place—understanding the professional advice needed, marketing, finances and people management—ensuring you have a secure foundation from which to launch your business.

Day 2

Establishing your business

Key areas we will cover on day 2:

▶ filing

▶ organising licences, permits, registrations and certificates

▶ choosing a business structure and business name

▶ considering a franchise

▶ business planning

▶ exit strategies.

Good morning and welcome back. How are you feeling after yesterday? Do you feel ready to start a business? Following on from yesterday, today we will be looking at the various government formalities your business will need to consider—yes, the hairball that is known as red tape. In Australia, government at all three levels—federal, state and local—has regulations in place that your business may need to comply with and it is your responsibility to understand them and work towards compliance. We will discuss the areas related to establishing a business, from the fun aspects of choosing a business name through to the tough decisions about legal structure and where the business will call home. As well as the compliance issues, we will discuss financing issues such as whether the business needs an investment to start up, and from where it will source its initial financing. I will also talk about the benefits of writing a business plan, and show you how you can organically create a business plan over seven days. In fact, if you completed the activities on day 1 you have already started.

Filing

As you start your business you will find you accumulate lots of information and documents, some of which you will need to read, and some that you will need to keep for future reference. You could purchase an accordion file (this is Officeworks's most popular stationery item!) and set up a filing system. Or you could minimise storage space by filing documents digitally, as I do. You can do this on your own computer, ensuring that it is regularly backed up. I use Carbonite (www.carbonite.com.au). Alternatively you could use an online storage solution such as Dropbox (www.dropbox.com) or Evernote (www.evernote.com).

To ensure your filing is kept simple, it's a good idea to use the same category names across your accordion files, computer file directory and email folders. Figure 2.1 shows some suggested category names.

I do not keep duplicate documents and my preference is to store the documents digitally (with a back-up system in place).

Figure 2.1: suggested categories for paper and digital filing systems

Accordion file	File directory	Email folder
ADMINISTRATION PRODUCT/SERVICE* FINANCE LEGAL MARKETING PEOPLE	C:\BUSINESS\ ADMINISTRATION PRODUCT/SERVICE FINANCE LEGAL MARKETING PEOPLE	Inbox: BUSINESS ADMINISTRATION PRODUCT/SERVICE FINANCE LEGAL MARKETING PEOPLE

*This category may be broken down further to suit your needs.

Licences, permits, registrations and certificates

One of the joys of going into business is discovering the plethora of licences, permits, registrations and certificates you are required to obtain at a federal, state and local government level—from business name registration, to food permits and everything in between. It can be quite overwhelming, but many of these requirements are in place to protect you and your customer.

For example, when you purchase food, you assume it has met certain hygiene standards. To meet these standards, employees must be trained in health and safety and in using the correct cleaning equipment. As the employer of a food-vending business you would have to allow time and money for this training (and for checking that your employees are adhering to the standards). You would also have to ensure you have regular pest inspections and that all fire regulations are met (including purchasing extinguishers, blankets and cut-off switches). You would expect that your competitors are also adhering to these hygiene and safety standards and that their expenses and administrative burdens are the same as those of your business.

There is a central online area at www.govforms.business. gov.au where you can register for free and locate, manage and complete government forms. You may be aware of what government paperwork you require, but it is still worth contacting your local, state and federal governments directly to ensure you have covered all bases. For example, in Queensland you can visit an interactive website called SmartLicence: www.sd.qld.gov.au/dsdweb/htdocs/slol. After answering numerous questions about your business, you will be provided with a summary of the government requirements applicable to your business. Table 2.1 lists the websites you can visit to obtain the necessary information.

Table 2.1: state government offices for licences, permits, registrations and certificates

State	Website
ACT	Canberra Connect www.canberraconnect.act.gov.au
NSW	NSW Government Licensing Service www.licence.nsw.gov.au/FAQ.htm
NT	Northern Territory Government www.nt.gov.au
Qld	SmartLicence: www.sd.qld.gov.au/dsdweb/htdocs/slol
SA	Consumer and Business Services www.ocba.sa.gov.au
Tas.	Service Tasmania Online www.service.tas.gov.au
Vic.	Business Victoria www.business.vic.gov.au
WA	Department of Commerce www.commerce.wa.gov.au/index.htm

Remember that if you are operating in more than one state or country you will need to contact all of the governments directly to ascertain what your business must comply with.

Activity 2.1

What licences, permits, registrations and certificates does your business potentially require? (Include a table of what you have and what you will need.)

Registering for an ABN

An Australian Business Number, otherwise known as an ABN, is a unique, 11-digit identification number used by the government to identify businesses.

The process of registering for an ABN is insanely simple. Many people think it is actually too simple and individuals register for an ABN without doing their due diligence; that is, without understanding what they are committing to. Registering for an ABN does not automatically register your business name. That process is done separately.

You can pay a professional—such as your accountant or lawyer—to register your business for an ABN, or you can save money and register it yourself by visiting www.abr.gov.au. The process is free.

Registering for an ABN is not compulsory. However, if you are operating as a business, there are benefits to registering. You are required to have an ABN if you want to register for the GST and for certain dealings with the Australian Taxation Office (ATO). If you issue an invoice without an ABN to a business, that business is currently obliged to withhold 46.5 per cent PAYG tax from their payment and submit it directly to the ATO on your behalf. Likewise, when you are in business you will need to do the same. You require an ABN to purchase an Australian **domain name** (.com.au) and to claim some government incentives. Businesses will also use your ABN as a means of verifying your business's identity. If you have an ABN you have to display the number on your invoices.

Your ABN may incorporate your nine-digit Australian Company Number (ACN). Under the *Corporations Act 2001* every company must be issued with an ACN. Not all businesses will be formed as companies, so you may not have an ACN.

Activity 2.2

- What is your registered ABN?

- What is your ACN?

Choosing a business structure

When you begin contemplating the legal structure for your business it helps to start with the end in mind. How do you perceive your association with the business ending? Are you hoping to sell it, leave it to your children as an inheritance, franchise it, sell the shares in the business, list the business on the stock exchange or simply close the business down and sell off any assets? Thinking about how you want to leave the business will actually assist you in answering many questions about starting your business. Choosing how to set up the legal structure of your business is an important decision. Each state has different laws and you will need to spend some money and consult with professionals — namely your accountant and your lawyer — for specific advice suited to your needs.

There are four different business-structure options:

▶ sole trader

▶ partnership

▶ proprietary limited (Pty Ltd) company

▶ trust.

When deciding which one is right for you, you should consider how tax is applied to the business, the protection of assets, your operating costs, how other businesses may deal with you and who owns the business.

Sole trader

As the name suggests, a sole trader basically operates on their own. The option is cheap and simple, but it may leave your personal assets exposed if difficulties arise. If someone sues you as a sole trader, your personal assets may be at risk.

Partnership

This structure involves sharing the responsibility of the business between two or more people. The partnership contract needs to very clearly define every aspect of the partnership agreement: the roles and responsibilities of each partner, how income will be distributed, how the workload is distributed and how the partnership will end. Professions such as accounting and law typically opt for a partnership business structure.

As you start out in your business you may go into some form of business relationship with your friends—maybe as a partner, supplier or customer. At the outset it may seem like a great idea to go into business with someone you socialise with, can talk with and know well. It gives you the opportunity to spend more time with them and work together on something that you are passionate about. However, I have seen business owners discover that their friends aren't as skilled in their business abilities and responsibilities as you thought they were going to be. They don't have the same drive and commitment to see the business succeed, yet they expect to reap the same rewards. Going into business with your friends can be difficult for all involved because you may wear emotional glasses and not see their true performance in the business. As the business relationship strains, financial pressures mount, social situations become awkward and the potential success of the business is affected.

If you decide to go into business with a friend, you need to establish very clearly defined parameters around the business relationship. You both need to agree on professional and acceptable terms for ending the relationship to ensure a business failure does not also lead to the end of your personal relationship. If you are contemplating going into business with a friend, talk to others in the social circle about your ideas. Do they think you will work well together? Some friends work really well together in business; they respect each other and they bring different skills to the business. Other friends may be great social buddies, but may have different business values and work ethics, which is unlikely to cement a long-term business relationship. You don't want to find out your best mate is completely incompetent when it comes to business, and that you are basically supporting two families.

Proprietary limited company

The proprietary limited (Pty Ltd) company option gives you a lot more protection because the business is a separate legal entity. If anyone sues your business, they can only sue the assets of the business; they cannot sue your personal assets. There are additional costs and reporting requirements associated with setting up and running a Pty Ltd business.

> **Activity 2.3**
>
> - What is the chosen legal structure of the business?
> - Who will have ownership of the business?

Trust

A trust is not a separate legal entity like a Pty Ltd company, nor are you the sole trader. It is a legal relationship, or the mediator between a trustee and a beneficiary. It is set up through a trust deed to protect the assets for the benefit of the trust beneficiary. There are different types of trusts: unit trusts, discretionary trusts (such as a family trust) and hybrid trusts. The features of a trust include the streaming of income or losses, limited liability and there may be taxation benefits. The administration of a trust is complicated and professional assistance may be required in the management of the trust.

Date of commencement

The date the business commences is typically determined by the date you register for an ABN. Various factors may assist you in deciding when you want the business to commence: the target market, the season, the economy and the financial year end. In Australia the financial year ends on 30 June so if you are planning on starting a business close to that date it may be wiser to hold off until the new financial year. That way you can avoid the administrative hassle of submitting company returns and activity statements to the ATO for a relatively short period of time.

The business name

Choosing a business name can be a significant milestone in the creation and setting up of your business, although it is often not an easy task and there are many factors to consider.

Your business name needs to be original, legally available and it must represent you and your business for many years to come. There are two parts: choosing a business name and registering a business name. First I will talk about the boring yet important aspect of registering a business name.

The reason I want to talk about this first is I want you to have an appreciation of the cost and administrative burden involved in choosing a business name, and the complications involved in unwisely choosing a name. If you opt not to have a business name, and simply do the work as 'Joe Smith the graphic design artist' you do not have to pay to register or **trademark** a name. However, this may limit the growth of your business. If you go through the registration process and change your mind it is a costly and time-consuming process.

Registering a business name

Registration for business names is managed at a national level by the Australian Securities and Investments Commission (ASIC). Once registered, the business name is registered nationally. National registration for one year costs $30 and for three years it costs $70. Visit www.business.gov.au/registerbusinessname for more information. If the business name includes the business owner's first name and surname, then the business name does not need to be registered. If you are in doubt check with ASIC (www.asic.gov.au), who should be able to advise you.

Choosing a business name

When you are choosing a business name there are some practical tips worth contemplating:

▶ *Don't choose a name that limits your business.* As mentioned before, you need to start with the end in mind. Are you starting your business with the intention of selling it down the track? If you name your business after yourself but you plan to sell, you may consider a more generic name. (Of course, Colonel Sanders, John Deere and Mrs. Fields would disagree with that advice!) If, however, your business is associated with a celebrity, you may well incorporate their name in the business to leverage off the celebrity association.

Another reason for using a generic name is that although you probably have a good idea what your business intends to do in its first year, it may evolve so a specific name is no longer suited. Colonial Sugar Refineries (CSR), for example, has expanded its operations to building products and aluminium. What a business may start doing and what it ends up doing may be totally different.

▶ *Emphasise the qualities and brand you want to promote.* Your business name says a lot about your brand. Using words such as 'bi-lo', 'discount', 'cheap' or 'luxurious' when naming your business ensures customers know something about your prices. Likewise, you could emphasise nationality, sustainability or another aspect of the business that you want to promote. You may choose to emphasise the suburb, city or state you reside in and encourage the community to shop locally, or you may choose to target a more global audience.

▶ *Make your name easy to spell and pronounce.* If someone hears the business name on the radio, can they google the name and find the business? I failed at this one, as many people seem to struggle to say my business name, 'ANISE Consulting'. I have practically stopped using it.

▶ *Set yourself apart.* Before you decide on a name, run it through various search engines on the internet. Are there other businesses with similar names here in Australia or overseas? Or is the name too general; for example, 'Exotic Cars' or 'Healthy Fitness'. Business names such as these can be almost impossible to find on the internet even if you know exactly what you are looking for.

▶ *Are you allowed to use the selected words in your business name?* It is unlikely that you can use a trademark name in your business. The business that owns the trademark and has built the brand reputation has the right of ownership and usage over the name. For example, MYOB is a trademark term and no business is allowed to use it in their business name. So even though I am a MYOB Certified Consultant I cannot set up a business called 'Heather's MYOB Consultancy Services'! In Australia we had an interesting case related to this. A US-based company trademarked the term 'ugg boots'. Here in Australia we consider the term 'ugg' boots to be a generic term, so while the term cannot be used in a business name overseas it can be used here in Australia.

▶ *Do you want to sound like your competitor?* Make a list of all of your competitors. Do you want to sound like them or do you want to be distinguished from them? Sounding too much like a competitor can have consequences. For example, a client of mine ran a business in a county of England and a business with a similar sounding name started up nearby. My client would often receive purchase orders on his fax machine that were intended for the other company. He would then source the equipment and sell it to them, making a tidy profit!

▶ *Be passionate when choosing a name.* If you have a passion or an inspiration from somewhere else, use it. Explaining why you chose your name can attract people to your business and to your enthusiasm. For example, 'Surfers Café', 'Bondi Bleach Hairdressers' and 'Sundrenched Boats' are all great names for someone who likes the beach.

Once you have decided on a new business name go to the Australian Business Register (www.abr.business.gov.au) and see if any other business has a similar name.

Google your chosen business name and review the results. Is there anything in the search results that may have a negative impact on your business name? If there are more than 100 000 results, it is unlikely you will get to the top of Google's home page with the name you have chosen because it is so similar to existing names on the web.

Go to a site such as www.knowem.com or www.namechk.com to check if the name of your choice is available across popular digital and social media platforms. We will talk about social media on day 4, but it is important to understand availability before you commit to a business name.

In the internet age, where online marketing is so important, naming your company using a word that is descriptive of the service you offer—and therefore lends itself to a

uniform resource locator (URL) that can add weight to search engine optimisation — is a good idea.

What are the key words that people would use to find your business? If you can incorporate those terms into your business name, and then find out if the business's **web domain** is available for purchase, your ranking on search engines will be improved.

Brainstorming names

If you are lucky, a business name may randomly come to you while you are in the shower, doing yoga, running a marathon or drinking! However, for many of us that does not happen, and we agonise over choosing a business name. Over the years I have picked up some tips that may assist you in creatively brainstorming a business name.

▶ Crowdsource by asking a mass of people on social media channels you are associated with to share ideas with you.

▶ Run a competition on your Facebook page.

▶ Use a tool such as Thinkmap's 'Visual Thesaurus' (www.visualthesaurus.com), which returns a plethora of word options from a single word and play random word association games.

▶ Get out a whiteboard and markers and start brainstorming. Play with the words and make a shortlist of suitable candidates.

▶ Try an online business-name generator such as Wordlab (www.wordlab.com/gen/business-name-generator.php), WriteExpress (www.rhymer.com/naming.html) or Dot-o-mator (www.dotomator.com).

▶ Brainstorm with colleagues and friends you trust.

Your business name is just waiting for you to discover it!

Is there a story behind the business name you choose? Your customers will be interested in knowing why you chose your business name; it is part of your business story. I chose the name ANISE Consulting for my business because I liked the connotations of the word anise: it represents a star, a spice and a network, making it positive and interesting.

Activity 2.5

What will your registered business name be?

Activity 2.6

Does your business name have a story behind it?

Trademarks

A trademark is a way of legally protecting assets of the business, such as the business name or products the business brings to the market. The trademark can be sold or licensed to other businesses. Interestingly the same word can be trademarked by different businesses operating in different industries, as the perception is they are not competing with one another. A **wordmark** is a graphical representation of the company's name, and it can be legally protected in a similar fashion to a trademark. Even if you have a registered business, or domain, name this does not mean the name is trademark protected. Another business can come along after your business has been publicly using the business name, trademark the business name and prevent your business from using it. Neglecting to trademark or wordmark your business name can be a costly and expensive exercise.

You can register your business's trademark yourself, or you can engage an expert, such as a trademark attorney, to register the name for the business. To find out further information about trademarks, and to undertake a preliminary search of existing trademarks registered in Australia, contact the government agency IP Australia at www.ipaustralia.gov.au. On the IP Australia website you can access the Australian Trade Mark On-line Search System (ATMOSS) and search the database of pending and registered trademarks.

Activity 2.7

- Is your chosen business name available on the IP Australia website database, ATMOSS?

- Do you have a business name that must be trademarked?

Funding the initial investment

Where is the money coming from to start your business? Some business owners start and run their business on the smell of an oily rag. They are very frugal in their spending, they do not believe in borrowing and they reinvest the revenue back into the business.

If you do need to start your business with an initial injection of money there are a variety of options, including the following:

▶ *Personal funds*. If you believe in yourself you can dip into your own savings or an existing mortgage loan.

▶ *Bank loans*. Depending on the economic climate you may be able to apply to the bank for a bank loan to start your business. Your commitment will be to pay back the interest to the bank as it is due. As long as you are able to pay the bank back you will retain full ownership of the business. I have heard of business owners struggling to get bank loans initially to start their business who thought creatively and got a bank loan for a car, rather than a business. Another method, which I am *not* endorsing, is to fill out multiple credit-card application forms and submit them at the same time. This generates a line of credit, but credit-card interest rates are high and these types of loans can be very difficult to service.

► *Family, friends and fools.* This is the triple F of funding. You may be able to borrow money from your friends and family. The repayment terms may be less onerous than those of a bank, but if they need the money back, you may find yourself in an awkward position. As long as you are able to pay your family and friends back you will retain full ownership of the business.

► *Venture capital.* Commonly known as VC, this form of funding is where money is pooled to finance the early stage of fast-growing innovative start-up companies that are perceived to have great potential, and thus carry with them high risk. Venture capital companies offer this sort of funding, but it is typically extremely difficult to access. If you do wangle an invite to present to a VC firm to request funding, you will need to have a comprehensive business plan, including competitor analysis and a detailed financial forecast ready for them to review.

► *Angel funding.* An angel investor is a wealthy person who invests their own funds in a start-up business, usually in exchange for equity in the business. This means you would no longer have full ownership and control of the business. However, in Australia angel investment is extremely rare. If you are a technology start-up company you may have better luck spending time in the coffee shops of Palo Alto building networks and working towards an introduction to a venture capitalist.

► *Government grants.* The government at a federal and state level offers hundreds of grants, loans and subsidies as well as low-interest loans that your business may be able to apply for. The Grants & Assistance Finder (www.business.gov.au/Grantfinder/Grantfinder.aspx) is a tool with which small business owners can search for various funding options.

► *Crowd funding.* Crowd funding is an innovative method of sourcing funds for investing into a business venture. It is an open call to the community, typically the online community, to present your business concept and request financial contributions to help start your business. It is a relatively new financing concept that works when many people donate a small amount of money. In return, contributors may get anything from a 'thank you' to some products or services when the business commences. If you are interested in the concept and have lots of friends with loose change in their pockets, visit www.indiegogo.com, www.pozible.com or www.kickstarter.com to see how it works.

If you are prepared to accept funding into your business venture you need to be very clear what the terms of the investment are. What are their expectations of you? Will you have to relinquish control? Will they bring in their own team to manage the business? Will they become shareholders and, if so, will they have the right to issue further shares, thus diluting your own holding? **Seed funding** from outside sources can enable you to grow your business faster, but it can also result in mistakes being made faster! You need to be very clear what you want from funding and what you are prepared to give up for it.

Franchising

A franchise is an arrangement where a franchisor leases a business model to a franchisee. The franchisor documents the processes of its own business and then licenses the business model to a franchisee. The franchisee has ownership in the success of the business. The franchisor offers varying levels of support, which typically will be reflected in the licensing costs.

A franchise can be a great way to start a business safely if you have the money to invest in purchasing a business. Buying into a franchise does not, however, guarantee business success. If you are planning to purchase a franchise, you need to do your due diligence and understand the commitment, involvement and support that will come from the franchisor, as not all franchises are created equal. You need to appreciate the state and federal laws governing franchises and you need to be clear about your own involvement in the business. Talk to other franchisee holders, speak with the Franchise Council, attend seminars and research your choices.

Ideally a franchise should be the perfect way to start a business. The processes are in place, and the promotional activity is planned and guided by the franchisor.

As with anything, when you buy into a franchise you need to ensure that you are comfortable with the relationship that you are committing to. The franchisee must comply with the franchisor's branding and model, which you may feel will stifle your own personal innovation. I have heard it said that the best owners of franchise models are those leaving armed services because they are very disciplined and focused and will follow the processes given to them without question. Entrepreneurs do not buy into the franchise model; business owners buy into the franchise model.

For a minimal investment you may also consider venturing into a network marketing business or a multilevel marketing business such as Amway, Avon or Tupperware. You sell their products and they typically provide extensive promotional and business support.

The distinction between franchising and network marketing is that a franchisee does not normally get compensated for introducing new people to the franchising model, while the network marketing model has commission benefits and is somewhat reliant on new members being introduced to the model.

Strategic planning

Strategic planning is essentially an exercise of looking at the big picture, defining the objectives or vision of your business and developing strategies to reach those objectives. Strategic planning is not long-term planning. It is not analysing the completion of current tasks, and assessing how new tasks fit into the timeline. Strategic planning involves taking a step back and looking at your business, the resources available to your business and the external environment in which the business is operating.

To a small business owner the thought of undertaking strategic planning can be daunting, overwhelming, time consuming and unnecessary. But what are the alternatives? Hard work, hard work, hard work! It is very easy to confuse hard work with success, but look around you: there are a lot of people running very fast on the business treadmill, but not necessarily achieving financial freedom. Without some thought about the strategic plan of your business, your operations will remain stagnant, in limbo, heading in an undefined direction, and you will be reactive rather than proactive.

The strategic planning process

The strategic planning process can be defined in five steps.

1 *Vision.* Establish the vision for the business.

2 *Where are we now?* Recognise where the business is at right now.

3 *Where do we want to be?* Identify where the business wants to be.

4 *Gap analysis.* Analyse the gap between where the business is now and where the business wants to be.

5 *Strategies for bridging the gaps.* Develop strategies to get from where the business is now to where the business wants to be.

This process does not happen overnight, and businesses have sub-strategies that fall in line with their overall business strategy such as financial, marketing and staffing strategies.

Advantages of strategic planning

For a start, writing down plans and strategies is very cathartic. It is a weight off your shoulder to have your thoughts and ideas down on paper. The process involves taking time to look at the external environment you are operating in. You will also need to spend time identifying the business's core strengths and assessing its weaknesses. Strengths should be capitalised upon, and weaknesses are an opportunity for improvement.

Once you have the first draft of your strategic plan, you can present it to your business advisory board (which we will discuss on day 3). Together you can review it, comment on it, question your rationale, identify omissions and seek clarity. The other activities undertaken by the business should be mapped against the strategic plan to ensure the focus and direction of the business is maintained.

The business plan

A business plan is essentially a plan of what you intend to do with the business. It details why you are going into business, what goals you hope to achieve and how you hope to achieve those goals. It should be a comprehensive overview of every aspect of your business, and should clarify what the business aims to achieve. It can be an internal document or an external document. If the business requires investment from banks, partners or investors they are likely to want to see a business plan, and they may have their own format requirements. A business plan demonstrates that you have thought through all aspects of your business. It should not sit locked away in a desk drawer; it can be an integral part of your business—a living, breathing document that evolves with your business, especially during the start-up stage. You need to identify key data that you can extract easily from the business plan as a measurement tool for the success of the business.

There is a lot of debate in the business world about whether you need a business plan or whether it is simply a waste of time. I think if you are planning to commit time and money in a business, then it is worth spending some time up-front writing down a plan for the business that clarifies the purpose of the business. If you are not prepared to do this, should you be going into business? It is also likely to assist you in answering questions as you grow and evolve the business. It can be written on a single page or a comprehensive dossier. Brett Godfrey scribbled the business plan for the company he founded—Virgin Blue (later Virgin Australia)—on the back of 12 beer coasters. A business plan is what you make of it.

A business plan can be intimidating. Where do you start? What should it include? There is no set prescribed template for a business plan. The good news is that as you work through this book you will be presented with activities. If you answer the questions, by the end you will have the basis of a comprehensive business plan that will suit a small business.

I wrote my initial business plan over a two-week Christmas break, while staying in an isolated cottage in Maleny. I wrote and wrote and wrote. The process was very cathartic, and it gave me the foundation upon which I started my own business. Looking back at my original business plan, my business growth and purpose has almost mirrored the goals I set for myself in the written plan. I hope you too find working through the activities in this book, and developing your own business plan, a rewarding experience.

Exit strategies

Whoa! Am I reading the wrong book? I want to *start* a business, not stop a business. I know, but you need to think about an exit strategy at the start of your endeavour. This will actually assist you in making decisions that you will need to make along the way, such as agreements, goals and strategy planning for the enterprise.

The purpose of this discussion is to establish how you plan to smoothly transition out of the business. We will not address the mechanics of leaving a business, nor will we cover bankruptcy or insolvency, which are obviously not desirable outcomes to consider when starting a business.

There are a number of options for ending a business.

▶ *Close the business.* The business is wound up. The doors are shut. The ABN is cancelled, the ATO is notified and the business stops serving clients. No money has been made from the sale of the asset, the business entity, but the business owner can contemplate selling other assets, such as furniture and fixtures, domain addresses, the client list and potential future sales.

▶ *Sell the business.* The business and all its assets and liabilities are sold. You may use a business broker who sells businesses depending on the size of the business, and the owner and employees may stay in the new business for a handover period of time. The business owner receives payment for the sale. The new owner may run the business as it was, integrate it with their existing business or shut it down completely so as to eliminate competition from the market.

▶ *List the business.* The business is listed on the stock exchange. The company ownership is divided into shares, and these shares are made available for the public to purchase on the stock exchange. This is an expensive and complex process and fewer companies are taking their business to be listed on the stock exchange; instead they may integrate with an already exiting company. Typically this is a method whereby business owners make a large amount of money.

▶ *Leave the business as an inheritance.* The business is passed to another family member. This can be done as an inheritance or as an arrangement while the owner is living. If you intend to leave the business as an inheritance you need to consider if the recipients want the business. If you leave the business to three children, but only two of them want to manage the business, they will be left with the financial burden of buying the third sibling out of the business, which may not be an ideal situation.

▶ *Give the business away.* Yes, this does actually happen. The original business owner simply gives the business away. Perhaps due to a significant event in their life, they are unable to continue with the business and don't have the time to deal with other options, and they give the business away. This is unlikely to be part of your succession strategy, as no money will be earned from giving the business away.

Obviously the answer to how you want to leave the enterprise may evolve through the life of your business, but it is good to have a plan in place for how you envisage the end to be, to ensure you maximise its value. Throughout the life of the business you also need to be aware of any business arrangements you partake in that may affect leaving it. For instance, if you sign a contract with suppliers or customers for the delivery of goods over a certain period of time, leaving the business may affect that legal arrangement and result in additional costs. Likewise, if staff have been employed and the business ends, there may be redundancy payments to deal with. Sometimes it can take many years to actually leave an enterprise, which may be an unwanted burden.

Summary of day 2

We have come to the end of day 2. You have probably been mulling over some of the aspects covered today for quite a while, such as a name for your business. There may be other areas, such as licensing and permits, that you were completely unaware of and that you have now put on your to-do list for further investigation. We have discussed some typical and novel ways to find initial financing for your business and after day 5 you will have a better idea of the financing you need for your business.

On day 3 we will discuss when you need to seek help from experts and professionals.

Day 3

Getting professional advice

Key areas we will cover on day 3:

▶ finding a small business specialist

▶ finding a lawyer

▶ financial requirements

▶ insurance requirements

▶ technology and software requirements

▶ telecommunications and sustainability considerations.

On day 3 we will discuss the different aspects of your business that will require you, as the business owner, to seek professional advice specific to your circumstances. This will ensure you have set up the business correctly, you are protecting your assets and you are meeting your legal and taxation obligations. Initially I will explore where to find and how to select a specialist for your business. Following on from that I will discuss various considerations related to starting your small business. There are many bodies offering small business assistance. It is essential that you understand their credentials, how they will be paid and how they can help you.

Selecting a specialist

I think before discussing the different types of specialists you may need, and why you may need them, it would be good to go through the process of how to find or select a specialist to assist you with your business. It is unlikely, especially in the early stages, that the specialist will work within the business. Typically they will consult into the business as and when you require and as your budget permits.

I worked with a client who, based on the advice of his bookkeeper's boyfriend, implemented a point-of-sale system in his stores throughout Queensland. The system was an unruly monster. It was not GST compliant, and the decision meant the company had several hard years of struggling through the implementation, realising the system was wrong and working to get a new system. I always say that successful businesses consistently make the right decisions for the business. Choosing the right specialist, listening to their advice and taking from it what you need to make a decision that is right for your business is an essential part of business success. Hopefully working through some of these considerations will help you find the right person to give advice to your business.

Here are a few suggestions for finding a specialist.

▶ Depending on what you are looking for, each state or territory is likely to have an industry body that you can contact to find their members' location, specialities and contact details.

▶ Ask people working in a similar industry for suggestions.

▶ Look on the internet, as specialists don't need to live next door. Through the power of technology, I support businesses across the world, and you too may find the support you need at the other end of your computer.

▶ Ask around your network for recommendations. Ask your professional network on LinkedIn, or your friends on Facebook.

▶ Be aware that some people receive inducements for recommendations, so they are not necessarily offering the recommendation because they have used the specialist or know their work, but because there is a financial incentive involved.

▶ In contrast to specialists who take inducements for recommendations, some will only take on new clients who are pre-approved by way of a referral. In my experience, many of the best accountants' books are full, and this is the way they operate: they want the client (you) vetted so they know you will be a good match for the business.

What to look for

If you have the luxury of a choice of specialists, here are some general questions you should consider when choosing an expert. Obviously you may need to tailor them for your particular situation.

▶ Does the specialist have the qualifications or accreditations necessary to provide expert advice?

▶ Does the specialist understand the industry you operate in?

▶ Does the specialist understand small business? While someone may be highly experienced in their given field they may not understand the nuances of small business.

▶ Do you understand the specialist? Do they speak using a language you understand?

▶ Does the specialist communicate with you using appropriate means? Are they available to take your calls, respond to your emails and answer your questions? I recall calling a lawyer when I needed one for my business and she said she guaranteed to return calls, and would not leave the office until all of the day's emails and phone calls had been dealt with. Impressive commitment, but my concern for her own personal work-life balance meant I never called her again. I guess I am too nice, and perhaps a more ruthless person would have been attracted to that commitment. Once you are engaged with the firm, will you speak with other staff, or will you deal directly with the specialist? I have been told by many clients that their accountant was available in the early days but over the years the practice grew and the accountant was never available and never returned calls.

▶ What and how do they charge? You need to clarify up front how much they will charge. Is it a standard fee or an hourly rate? Is it within your budget? Specialists' expenses can be exorbitant so be clear about what you are committing yourself to.

▶ How old are they? If you invest time in finding a specialist and you are planning to have a long-term relationship with them, it may be good if they are about your age or younger than you. I realise that sounds ageist; however, I know of a number of businesses who dealt with a lawyer or accountant who retired, and they then had the hassle of extracting themselves and finding another specialist.

If I was looking for assistance I would customise the questions to suit the situation and email the questions to a few businesses to gauge their responses. With all of these aspects to consider, you also need to be aware that your business needs may change and evolve, and you may need to move on from a very good specialist to another one more suited to your growing business. Most specialists do not provide services from microbusiness through to corporate giants, and who knows where your business may end up!

Legal requirements

A lawyer can help your business get the basics correct from the very beginning, assisting the business by developing clear, unambiguous, watertight contracts and agreements. During the start-up phase of your business, you will find that many of the decisions you make are formalised by way of a contract — a contract that you will want a lawyer to review and help you understand so that you understand what you are committing the business to.

A lawyer can assist with:

▶ setting up the business structure, including an exit strategy (it is worth noting that many tax accountants offer this service as well)

▶ registering business names and **intellectual property (IP)**

▶ preparing contracts for investors, suppliers, customers and employees

▶ negotiating commercial leases or rental agreements

▶ hire-purchase contracts.

As a business owner it is wise to avoid verbal arrangements, assumptions and misunderstandings. Commit to written agreements to ensure you understand the exact obligations you are undertaking. It can be overwhelming entering the world of negotiating your own business deals. From very small arrangements—such as buying a box of bananas—to lease agreements, you will come across people who will suggest you do not need the agreement in writing and that a handshake will do. Lawyers and legal fees are expensive. They can be a significant cash-flow drain in the early stages of business, and it is easy to try to avoid consulting with a lawyer to save you money in the short term. However, if something goes wrong—a partnership goes bad, a lease turns sour or someone tries to take advantage of you—you will be pleased that you invested in a lawyer.

Finding a lawyer

Each state has a Law Society and a Legal Aid centre. The Law Society will help you with details such as the location of lawyers, the areas of law that they specialise in and their accreditation. Legal Aid centres have information and may be able to point you in the right direction. However, they do not focus on helping someone who is starting a small business.

Activity 3.1

- What legislation may impact the running of your business?

- What areas of your business will you get a small-business lawyer to assist you with?

Financial requirements

A good accountant who spends time to really understand your business can improve profitability and save you considerable sums in taxes by ensuring the structure, business entity, income distribution and any investments you may have are arranged to suit the business and evolving tax environment.

Accountants are like doctors: there are many different specialisations among them. It is likely that you are familiar with tax accountants and perhaps when you think of an accountant, you think of a tax accountant.

A tax accountant or a registered tax agent prepares and lodges the business tax returns for the business. They may also offer additional services such as preparing and lodging activity statements, producing financial reports and assisting you with strategic financial growth advice for the business.

A management accountant uses the accounting information within the business to assist the business in strategic planning and making informed decisions about the business. They typically prepare regular management reports for the business. This is primarily the work that I do.

A registered BAS agent is authorised to prepare and lodge activity statements. Both the tax agent and the BAS agent need to be registered with the Tax Practitioners Board in Australia.

A bookkeeper may undertake the administrative duties of the accounting department, including data entry, from processing data through to the trial balance.

Depending on the size of your business, the accounts department may be within your business or it may be external to your business.

No matter who is undertaking the accounting role for your business, it may surprise you to know that at the end of day the business owner is responsible for what is submitted to the tax office. When you establish a relationship with an accountant, you sign a disclaimer that all information provided to them is correct, and that you are the person verifying the accuracy of the tax return.

If you employ someone within the business to undertake the accounting role, you may still have external accountants who undertake the tax submission role for the business.

Here are some further aspects you should consider when choosing an accountant.

▶ *How will they access your financial information?* Have they heard of the internet? Can they remotely connect to your data, or do they expect you to send them a zipped data file, or worse still paper copies of reports you produce?

▶ *What accounting software package does the accountant recommend?* Will it suit your business? If you are planning to use a different type of software, will they be able to work with it?

▶ *Will work be done onsite or remotely?* Will your business papers and data leave your office?

▶ *How will your accountant communicate with you?* Finding a good accountant, either internally or externally, is really hard. I think this is because of miscommunication: the business owner often does not understand what the accountant is going to do for them. They think the tax accountant will actively submit business tax returns, or a bookkeeper will actively chase debts, but there needs to be a clear understanding of roles and responsibilities to ensure a successful business relationship.

Activity 3.2

- Will you do the bookkeeping yourself, hire a bookkeeper or outsource bookkeeping?

- Will you do the tax accounting yourself or hire the services of a tax accountant?

- Do you want the tax accountant to assist only with basic taxation compliance or will they be a financial adviser to the business as well?

Finding trusted business advisers

There are many avenues through which you can seek business advice but it's important to ensure you can be confident in advice you receive.

Advisory boards

Your business may benefit from the insights and wisdom gained by implementing a formal or informal (read unpaid!) advisory board. A good quality advisory board can assist you in developing strategies, provide insight and open up doors for your business. You do not want 'yes' people on your advisory board who enthusiastically believe in every business idea you have! You want a broad range of opinions.

Business coaches

A business coach is someone who motivates you by asking probing questions, assisting you in setting measurable goals and helping you focus you on achieving those goals. They may not be skilled or experienced in the given field. The International Coach Federation Australasia (www.icfaustralasia.com) has an accreditation process and directory of business coaches who may be able to assist your business. Unfortunately, the business coaching industry is not regulated, and other than their own coaching business, the coach may never have run a business.

Business mentors

A business mentor is someone who has wisdom, experience and knowledge in a particular area and shares this with you. Mentoring is generally at a more personal level, and may not have prescribed outcomes.

If you were starting a hairdressing business, your business mentor would be an experienced expert in the hairdressing industry who can share insights and contacts with you, while a business coach helps you develop and set goals to stay motivated. The business coach may not necessarily have specific experience in the hairdressing industry.

Personal empowerment

As you start your business, take the time to read or listen to the plethora of business books on the market. There are theoretical business books and coffee-table, cutting-edge, business-wisdom books. If a book is recommended to me, I always add it to my LinkedIn profile of books I intend to read. This is an easy way to monitor books. I am time poor, but love to read, so I have adopted some strategies that may work for you.

▶ I listen to audio books. They are similar in price to a retail book. Many are between two and four hours long, and I gain wisdom while working out.

▶ I carry a huge handbag with me everywhere, and always have a book with me.

▶ I maintain a pile of disposable reading—magazines or books that, once read, I am happy to give away. Whenever I go anywhere that involves a waiting room, I grab something from the pile, read it and leave it in the waiting room for the next entrepreneur who comes along!

I have never read a book and not learned something beneficial from it, and part of my 'reduce, reuse, recycle' mantra means I don't hoard books. I am always reading them and then passing them on, sharing the wisdom.

Activity 3.3

- Would you benefit from the expertise of a business coach?

- Would you benefit from the expertise of a business mentor?

- Will your business have an advisory board? Who will be on it?

Insurance requirements

To get the momentum behind launching your own business you have to be overflowing with positivity. However, you also need to consider the risks that could impact your business. Natural disasters, injury, sickness and theft are some of the risks that could occur. To manage risk within your business you need insurance. Insurance provides protection for your business and personal investments and gives you peace of mind, and your customers may require it before they will do business with you. Some industries will expect you to demonstrate that you have adequate insurance before they will include you on their preferred supplier list and some professional organisations may also require you to demonstrate that you hold professional indemnity insurance.

There are numerous types of insurance coverage available for your business. You can source them directly yourself or seek the expertise of an insurance broker. Unfortunately, you may find you need to deal with several insurance brokers to cover the full spectrum of your business and personal insurance needs—from small business through to personal requirements. As a small business owner you will not have the security of being employed, the sick-day buffer or company health coverage. You will need to contemplate all sorts of insurance, such as additional personal insurance in case you fall ill or income protection in case you cannot work. I am a bit obsessive about risk management and being overly prepared. I have counted that within my family unit we have more than 20 different types of insurance.

Here are some business insurances you should consider.

▶ *Public liability insurance.* This insurance covers a third party from death or injury. So, for example, if someone visits your premises and trips and injures themselves, the insurance covers them.

▶ *Professional indemnity insurance.* This covers you if you offer professional advice and someone sues you as a result of the advice you offer.

▶ *Product liability insurance.* This covers you for legal action as the result of injury, damage or death from a product.

▶ *Business asset insurance.* This insurance covers the business assets in the event of fire, burglary or damage.

▶ *Business revenue insurance.* Also called key person insurance, this covers you in situations where the business cannot operate (for example, due to fire or flood) and you are unable to trade or earn money for a period of time.

▶ *Tax audit insurance.* This insurance covers the cost of engaging your accountant and other professionals to assist in complying with an ATO audit or government compliance investigation.

▶ *WorkCover.* This insurance cover is mandatory if you have employees. It is one of the easiest insurances to navigate as it has an intuitive online website that steps you through the processes.

WorkCover is state or territory based and is coordinated by a government body. You pay WorkCover a set amount and if an employee makes a claim they deal with WorkCover. You provide WorkCover with an estimate of your employees' salaries at the beginning of the period, and pay an insurance amount based on that estimate. If the estimate goes up or down significantly you can adjust it during the period.

Insurance is another area that it is worth speaking to your industry body about. They may well be able to suggest an affiliated insurance company that in turn can offer you insurance focused on your needs, at a discount. I am a member of an association and the insurance I can access because of my membership is considerably cheaper than I can obtain in the open market.

Activity 3.4

- Circle the insurances will you need to consider for your business:

  public liability   professional indemnity
  product liability   business assets
  business revenue   workers' compensation
  tax audit.

- Complete this risk-management table.

What risks could impact on your business?	How will you minimise possible risks to the business?

Intellectual property considerations

If within your business you are going to develop intellectual property (IP)—an invention, trademark, design or a practical application of your idea—you may need to speak with an expert about commercialisation or protection of your IP. You will also need to consider implementing confidentiality agreements with anyone who may be working on the project. The government organisation, IP Australia (www.ipaustralia.gov.au) has extensive information and support for businesses in this area.

Activity 3.5

- Will your business have intellectual property?

- How will you protect your intellectual property?

- Do you intend to have designs, patents or trademarks that you will need to register appropriately?

- Do you need to put non-disclosure agreements in place?

Technology considerations

Technology will free up your time to work on your business. Investing in technology will improve productivity, reduce administrative tasks, enable change in the business, reduce costs and create a competitive advantage. In today's environment your small business will need to consider and invest in information technology (IT) support and hardware. You may be able to leverage off your existing technology as you bootstrap your business start-up and build purchases into the businesses budget. Many suppliers offer financing or leasing for technology purchases, which may be an option you wish to consider—but make sure you're aware of the interest charges involved.

Here's a list of the basic hardware your office may require:

▶ desktop or laptop computer

▶ printer

▶ shredder

▶ server.

Servers

As your business grows and you purchase more computers you need to look at having a network set-up so the computers can talk to one another via a server. Two options for doing this are:

▶ *Peer-to-peer network.* As the name suggests the computers are connected to one another as equals and there is no central controlling hub computer.

▶ *Server-run network.* The server is a dedicated physical computer that manages, stores, processes and sends data 24/7 to the other computers on the network.

Servers can be located in-house or in the clouds.

Activity 3.6

■ What hardware will you require for your business?

■ How will you procure it? (cash, credit or leasing)

■ How much will this cost you?

Software

Depending on the sort of business you are starting, you may need to invest in software—for example, email, word-processing and accounting software. I suggest you use products that are commonly available in the marketplace, so that you are able to communicate with people outside of your business. I recall a business using a home office suite that I had never heard of, and when they sent me emails I could not read them. They tried to convince me that I should use it as it was far better than Microsoft Office. However, if the software you use does not integrate with other businesses' management software, communication can be impaired. New staff members may also need to be trained in how to use the software, increasing business outlay. So it's a good idea to use something that has been universally adopted.

Cloud computing

As technology advances there is a move towards doing more business in the clouds and using cloud solutions. Essentially this means you process your work on the internet rather than on your computer and you subscribe to a service rather than purchase software and install it on your computer.

You may find if you are accessing the internet you are already using cloud services. Do you use internet banking, Gmail, Skype, Dropbox or Evernote? If the answer is yes you are already embracing **Software as a Service (SaaS)**. There are both benefits and concerns for running all or part of your business in the clouds.

Benefits of cloud computing

There are many benefits associated with cloud computing that businesses should be aware of; for example:

▶ *Cost savings*. You will save money as you don't need to purchase a server or invest in other infrastructure, and you won't require insurance over in-house hardware.

▶ *Productivity gains.* Many of the online services can speak to one another (with permission). This means that data entered at one spot will feed through to other applications so you don't need to re-key the data. For example, the transactions that happen with your online bank can feed into your accounting software and you don't physically have to enter the data. You will still, however, have to code the transaction. Being able to access your business data wherever you can access the internet means further productivity gains because being away from the office does not have to stop you working.

▶ *Mac or PC.* It does not matter what type of computer you choose as you access the information via a web browser such as Internet Explorer or Safari.

▶ *Convenience.* Online solutions are typically convenient; they can be accessed on mobile phones, tablet devices or wherever you can access the internet. They are also flexible and collaborative because other team members can log in and work on the same business information.

▶ *Price.* The cost can be lower than an outright software purchase. However, you may have ongoing monthly charges and you need to assess if that is a value-for-money proposition for your business.

▶ *Real-time data.* As the business information is all held in a central place, the data that you are looking at is the most up-to-date information the business has. For example, if you work on an Excel spreadsheet and send it to Jack, and he sends it to Charles, who sends it to Mary and then you want to do more work on it you will have no idea which version is the latest version. With online collaboration solutions, you are all working on the same version, so you never have to worry about this.

▶ *Security.* If your computer crashes, or you are flooded or affected by fires and you lose everything, your data is still available to go in the clouds. I am based in Brisbane and saw many clients affected by the floods of 2011. Paper records were destroyed and computer hardware was damaged beyond repair. Knowing that your data is secure in the clouds offers some comfort during such terrible ordeals. It is one less thing you have to concern yourself with.

▶ *Back-ups.* The solution provider will back up your data, so you don't have to invest in infrastructure to back it up (see my points about cost savings on p. 70). You also don't have to spend time doing back-ups (see my point about productivity gains on p. 71).

Concerns about cloud computing

I truly believe that cloud computing will become a standard part of doing business. However, it is worth noting there are presently some concerns about it so you need to consider and assess whether it is an appropriate solution for your small business.

▶ *Internet access.* You are reliant on internet access, so if you are in a regional area, cannot access the internet or have intermittent access to the internet it may not be the solution for you.

▶ *Slow access.* If the internet is slow, access is slow.

▶ *Storage.* Where is the business data stored? Is it in Australia or overseas? If it is overseas, which country's legislation governs that data storage? Typically, the storage will be maintained in several sites, so if one site is destroyed, for whatever reason, back-up data is accessible at another site.

▶ *Longevity.* Will the software provider be around to look after your data forever? Some cloud-based sites have already closed down and advised users to export all of their data as they would not be able to access it after a certain date. If, however, you actively choose to leave the provider, what will happen to your data? Will it be converted into read-only format and archived? Will you be able to download it?

▶ *Security.* The security encryption of your data is typically equivalent to a bank's security, but you need to assess the solution provider. If you are happy to do online banking, you should be happy with working in the clouds. You need to set up secure passwords so everyone accesses the information under their own username. It is also recommended that you encrypt or password protect your files while they are on your computer before sending them into the clouds (for example, before sending them to storage such as Dropbox). There are a variety of tools that can do this, such as Cloudfogger, SecretSync and BoxCryptor.

▶ *Ownership.* Some of the online solutions have business models in place so you, the end user, subscribe through a representative, rather than directly with the provider, and legally the representative owns your business data—not you. Yes, I was a bit startled to discover this and it is one of the questions you need to have answered and feel happy about.

▶ *Suitability.* Cloud computing is not suitable for all environments. If you want to collaborate on a huge file, such as an architectural drawing or a graphic design, uploading it to the web and working on it may be a very slow and intensive exercise.

Cloud computing is the future for business. Ten years ago we were worried about internet banking and purchasing online, and now it is a common activity. As time passes, many businesses will start to explore the possibilities of cloud computing. However, there are concerns, and if you choose a solution, you need to understand the terms and conditions you are agreeing to.

There are various places you can go to for IT support for your business. Many of the technology stores have informed staff and affiliated support services available to answer your questions. You may find when you purchase something you are entitled to onsite or remote support. When I purchased my DELL computer I was entitled to follow-up support with a business called Gizmo, which provides onsite and remote IT support for home and small offices. There are a number of businesses who offer charge-by-the-hour IT support as you need it, which is ideal for a small business. As you grow, you may want more consistent support, and outsourced IT support may serve your needs until the role is big enough to employ someone full time.

Activity 3.7

- What software do you require for your business?

- How much will it cost you?

Telecommunications requirements

Some days I sit in my office and my Skype phone starts ringing, my mobile phone starts ringing and my landline starts ringing. I regret promoting so many contact options when I started my business, as I have found it difficult to manage them all.

Some people have the philosophy that you should give clients as many ways as possible to contact you. However, when you throw email, DM (direct messaging) on Twitter and IM (instant messaging) on Facebook into the mix, it can be difficult to manage and coordinate responses. I also regret mixing my personal contact numbers with business contact numbers. I have found that clients call me astonishingly early in the morning, or on the weekend, and because I answer, they expect me to start helping them. This can be an awkward situation that, if I had thought it through at the start of my business, I could have managed better.

What contact number will you promote to the market? When should you be available to take business calls? When you are unavailable to answer business calls, who will answer and respond to incoming messages?

When you are establishing a business, there are several phone contact options available to choose from: landline, mobile, **VoIP** and 1300.

Telecommunications can have a big impact on your business's bottom line because it is a means of talking directly with your customers, and if used ineffectively can be an exorbitant expense. It is important that you develop suitable telecommunication strategies for your business.

Activity 3.8

- What contact number will you promote to the market?

- When will you be available to take business calls?

- When will you be unavailable to answer business calls?

- Who will answer and respond to incoming messages?

Sustainability considerations

Unless you have been hiding under your own carbon footprint you will realise that consumers are placing more emphasis on the environmental practices of who they are doing business with. Many micro- and home-based businesses are naturally eco-friendly. They take ownership of their surrounding work environment by driving less, and utilising emerging technologies and thriftiness out of necessity. As you are launching your business, it can be both economically and environmentally wise to think about adopting some earth-friendly practices, developing a sustainability policy and promoting green credentials to your potential new customers and the wider community.

Depending on the type of business you are planning to create, you may not need the services of a sustainability specialist. There are a lot of guidelines and resources available to the small business owner to assist them in developing a sustainability policy, and frankly it is common sense. However, many policy guides are oriented towards larger businesses that have a budget dedicated to maintaining sustainable work practices. As an example, some sustainable practices for a microbusiness could include:

► working towards a paperless office environment

► using technology such as Skype and **GoToAssist** to reduce car travel

► choosing green-friendly suppliers

► turning off equipment that is not being used

► utilising segregated recycling bins.

As you read this book and develop your business plan, keep note of the practical steps you are adopting, which you can then compile into your first draft of a sustainability policy.

Activity 3.9

- Will your business negatively impact the environment or local community?

- What environmental measures can your business adopt to ensure environmentally friendly behaviour?

Summary of day 3

As a business owner you are ultimately responsible for all aspects of the business. However, fortunately there are experts you can turn to who can help you establish, develop and grow your business. Empower yourself: understand how you can benefit from using the services of legal, accounting, technology, communication and human-resource experts in your business.

This book is focused on starting a company in Australia. It is certainly desirable and achievable to grow an international business. However, moving into a global market is complicated. You need to adhere to new rules, new cultures and new taxes. The experts you choose initially may not be the specialists you use as your business grows. Be open and adaptable to change.

Day 4

Marketing

Key areas we will cover on day 4

▶ developing a promotional calendar

▶ creating a recognisable brand for your business

▶ managing customer relations

▶ dealing with competitors

▶ email and newsletters

▶ offline and online marketing activities.

Today we are going to explore the basics of marketing. You need to get your potential customers or clients to open their wallets and actively buy your product or services and this will be done through marketing the business. We talked about the importance of market research on day 1, and this helped us understand who our market is, who may be a potential competitor, what the business environment will be like and how our products or services will be perceived by the market. Today we will develop a marketing calendar of activities, talk about the importance of developing your business's brand and establishing the foundation of offline and online marketing activity opportunities. In one day and in one chapter we cannot cover every aspect of marketing, but the aim is to give you a good foundation of what you should be thinking about, and how you can develop a marketing strategy that will enable your business to scale and grow over time.

Marketing strategy

Before you dive into marketing the business you need to develop a marketing strategy that considers all aspects of marketing and aligns with the overall business strategy.

The aspects of marketing that you should consider include the 5 Ps (adapted from E. Jerome McCarthy's four Ps of marketing):

▶ *Product or service.* What will the brand name be? How will it be packaged? What warranty will you offer? What repairs and support services will you offer? What safety ratings will the product or service meet?

▶ *Pricing.* What pricing strategy will you adopt? The demand for goods or services will be affected by the price. This is known as price elasticity. If you have the flexibility to set your own prices, research competitor pricing, speak with a pricing expert and test the market to understand the optimum price elasticity of your goods or service. Sensitise your customers to the value rather than the price to ensure you maximise profits. You need to consider whether you will be at the luxurious or cheap end of the market when you price your products or services. Will you offer early payment discounts? Will you offer seasonal sales?

▶ *Place.* What are the logistics behind delivering the product or service? What distribution channels will you use? This may include selling into retail shops using shipping companies or online distribution methods.

▶ *Promotion.* How will you let potential customers know about the products or services? What advertising, publicity, sales or marketing activities will you use?

▶ *Positioning.* How will your customers or clients perceive you in the marketplace?

Once your business has planned what it wants to achieve with its marketing, activities and tactics can be developed that align with the strategy.

The marketing calendar

As you establish the foundation of your marketing strategy you can prepare a monthly promotional calendar for the first year that the business operates.

The first step to developing a promotional calendar is to assess outside forces or seasonal fluctuations that will affect the sales so you can determine when you will need to ramp up promotions. A business that makes replica medals is likely to see a positive return on their promotional dollar investment leading up to ANZAC Day. Likewise, if you were selling umbrellas, you would expect to sell more in the rainy season. Businesses need to appreciate and plan for low and high seasons.

Figure 4.1 (overleaf) shows a simple six-month forecast for a bookkeeping business. The top row identifies the time periods of the campaign, month by month. This could be broken down into weeks, months or quarters. The second row reflects the seasonal fluctuations that the business anticipates. In the bookkeeper's calendar the workload is affected by the client's tax date obligations, so it is relatively easy to define. The third row is the theme for the month's activities. Some general themes will affect all businesses: Christmas, Easter, ANZAC Day, Mother's Day and Father's Day. There may also be specific themes related to the industry: a key date for a milliner, for example, would be the Melbourne Cup. The next few rows detail different promotional activities that can be undertaken. This bookkeeping business has planned for an additional promotional period during their anticipated quiet times.

Figure 4.1: six-month marketing forecast for a bookkeeping business

Month	January	February	March	April	May	June
Busy/ quiet	Quiet (many people are away on holidays and business)	Busy	Quiet	Busy	Quiet	Busy
Theme	Happy New Year	Qtr 2 BAS due	St Patrick's Day Check for common errors	April Fool's Day Easter Qtr 3 BAS due	Prepare for end of financial year	Payment summaries due End of financial year
Email	Very brief with picture	5 theme-related tips	5 theme-related tips	5 theme-related tips	5 theme-related tips	5 theme-related tips
Media				Press release to local radio station about preparing for the end of the financial year		
LinkedIn/ Twitter	Microblog theme content	Microblog theme content	Microblog theme content	Microblog theme content	Microblog theme content	Microblog theme content
Direct mail			Postcards with a St Patrick's Day Irish theme can be mailed to clients			

As you can see, planning ahead using a marketing calendar gives a business a clear picture of the preparation they should undertake to ensure their marketing strategy is on task.

Activity 4.1

- Will your business be affected by seasonal fluctuations?

- Are there any significant dates in the calendar when your business can anticipate higher than average sales? Will you have the capacity to deliver?

- Prepare a one-year marketing calendar for your business. Make a note of the estimated costs for the budget forecast.

Branding

Branding is about how your business is recognised. Typically it may be recognition of the business name (see day 2), or the logo or features of a product or service that you offer. Building a consistent brand nurtures deep, loyal relationships that people believe in. It is not necessarily about promoting the business. To assist in conceptualising your brand, you may align it with a well-known identity: Lady Gaga would represent an innovative, unpredictable youth brand, while George Clooney would represent a sophisticated, mature, tasteful brand. I align my own business brand with Mary Poppins. I channel the well-known nanny as I empower businesses. I help them when they need help and I am in the background when they can do it on their own. Branding extends to the colours, logos and fonts, and these are aspects of the business that you may enjoy choosing yourself, or you can turn to a style expert for guidance on a design.

Business colours

As part of the branding exercise you should choose a colour or colours for your business. Consistently using the same colours in all communication material and the products you offer will build and enhance your brand. If you google 'colour palette generator' or visit www.colorschemer.com/online.html you can create a complimentary colour scheme to assist you with this. You need to choose colours that are easily replicated online and in your email correspondence. Once you have selected colours, create a colour style guide that includes the CMYK, RGB and Hex colour references. Then, whenever you get something printed online or offline you can advise the printer of the exact colour style they should use.

Activity 4.2

What colours will you choose for your business?

Colour	CMYK (cyan, magenta, yellow, black)	RGB (red, green, blue)	Hex (hexadecimal)
e.g. Brown	C 0.0000 M 0.0000 Y 0.2000 K 0.6670	858568	#555544

Logo

A logo is a distinctive emblem used by a business to aid in market recognition and branding the business. A logo can be the name or the primary letters of a business or a symbol representing the business. The red cursive words that spell Coca-Cola are the company logo for Coca-Cola. You may decide to try to create your own logo, use a graphic designer or use a crowdsourcing graphic design website such as the Australian company 99designs (www.99designs.com.au), where you compile a design brief and create a contest. Designers compete to create a logo for the business and you select the winner. Your logo should complement the business colours that you have chosen.

When you are arranging to get a logo created, make sure you will own the rights over the logo once it is developed. You will also need the logo provided to you in various formats, for inserting into invoices, websites, emails and promotional material. I have dealt with businesses that paid for a logo design and then had to pay additional fees to have the logo reformatted so they could add it to their tax invoice.

Once you have a logo, and start venturing online registering your business details with other sites, you will find that you need the business logo **hosted** online somewhere. This can be arranged during the process of creating a website, but a quick alternative method is to load the logo to a site called Photobucket (www.photobucket.com). You can upload the business logo to this free site and they will create a URL, which you can use when you need to provide a URL for an online version of your logo.

Activity 4.3

What ideas do you have for a business logo?

Fonts

To demonstrate consistency in your business's brand, choose a single, easily read, popular font that can be used in all business communications such as websites, business publications, word documents and emails. Using a combination of fonts is messy and confusing. And a word of warning: if you choose an uncommon font it may be unpredictably converted in digital reproduction such as emails or internet browsers.

Activity 4.4

What font style will you choose for your business?

Customer relationship management

To understand your customers you need to capture as much information as you can about them (without stalking them—that would be both creepy and illegal!) To achieve this you need to maintain a database of information on your customers; that is, a customer list.

There are **customer relationship management (CRM)** tools that collect data and assist you in connecting with and understanding your customers, from a free Google spreadsheet option to a powerful online solution that through **application programming interface (API)** technology can integrate or 'communicate' with your other business management software. CRMs include Podio, SugarCRM, Batchbook, Salesforce, Zoho and youGROW, to name a few. Many options have a free trial period or a free 'lite' version for limited users and functionality. For more robust solutions, prices range up to $100 per employee per month. Features you should look for in a CRM include the ability to collaborate with other users, manage leads, track sales, analytically track hyperlinks, and social media integration. I would also be inclined to choose an internet-based CRM to ensure access is available on mobile devices.

Using a CRM can assist you in understanding where your customers are located, whether they will open their wallets for what you have to sell, what other issues they have and when they last purchased from you. This in turn can help you market to them. Many start-up businesses told me they could not invest in the training they needed. This was a driving force behind my decision to write *Learn MYOB in 7 Days*—to provide an affordable alternative to training. A CRM can help you identify areas to grow your business offerings by identifying and solving clients' problems.

With respect to the relationship you have with your customers or clients, you may need to establish parameters about who you will not engage as a customer or client. Learning where to draw the line is particularly helpful. Experience has taught me that a client who distracts you from your core business can lead to undue stress, unpaid bills, unsatisfied clients and the inability to take advantage of business opportunities.

You may be faced with a potentially good client, but discover they do not fit your current business operations because:

▶ you do not have the capacity to serve them

▶ their culture (for example, formal or corporate) does not suit your style

▶ they want deliverables that move away from your core business

▶ they don't appear to listen to your advice

▶ their business or what they want you to do conflicts with your code of conduct

▶ the geographical location would make it uneconomical to service.

If you are approached by a potentially good client who does not fit with your current business operations you can refer them to a competitor who may be better suited to their needs. This solution means that your business operations are not stretched, your competition is appreciative of the referral and the client is happy you were able to provide them with a workable solution. You may also be able to generate an extra revenue stream by offering referrals to trusted colleagues: a win-win situation for all.

Alternatively you may be approached by a potentially difficult client, with whom you don't want to work because:

► they present security or safety concerns

► they turn to litigation as a way of resolving issues

► they show signs of having cash-flow problems

► they make you feel uncomfortable or your intuition suggests you should avoid working with them

► you have heard unsavoury rumours about the organisation

► they complain about the work performed by a competitor you consider to be very reliable

► it would be illegal to serve them (for example, businesses that sell alcohol or cigarettes can't serve minors).

Once you've come to the realisation that the client may be potentially difficult to deal with, never burn bridges. Don't refer them to anyone, and bow out of the relationship gracefully with the simple suggestion that you don't have the capacity to serve them now. As your experience and business confidence grows, so will your ability to recognise clients you should say no to. Staying focused on the business vision will ensure your business develops to meet the goals you have for it.

It is far easier and cheaper to sell to an existing client than it is to sell to a new client. One of the biggest mistakes I made in my own business was not collecting data or maintaining lists of all the people I have worked with. Don't do as I do. Do as I say: start nourishing your client list now! A CRM can help you identify the services your customers may need from your business and encourage repeat business.

Email

Email is an important business communication tool. If you are using email for business purposes, make sure that the emails you send are suited to the brand of your business. Don't start sending business emails from silly email addresses you set up when you were a teenager. Higgilypiggily@gmail.com does not instil confidence in your business acumen.

As soon as you get a domain name for your business I encourage you to arrange to get a business email address attached to the domain name (mine is Heather@yourbusiness .com.au). You could do this through your internet provider or use an application called Google Apps. I use the free version of Google Apps. You need to be a bit technically savvy to use it, but once it is set up, you have access to web-based emails, calendars and documents (including word processing and spreadsheets). What I especially like is that it enables me to create and control email addresses for my business. If I work with a virtual provider, I can create an email address for them, and any communication they undertake on my behalf will have my brand associated with it. Ask your IT provider to set up your email so you know how to access it online, and so that emails download to your computer and sync to your mobile phone. Make sure you set it up so you can access and respond to your business emails anywhere (if you want to!).

Whether you are using an online email service or an email software program such as Microsoft Outlook, I encourage you to set up an automatic signature that will appear on all new emails and responses. The automatic signature should include clear contact details, and take the opportunity to promote current services and inspire the recipient to sign up to your business newsletter. All business representatives should use a customised mirror version of the signature to instil brand consistency. I would discourage setting up the entire email as a graphic logo; some people only receive emails as text, and all the information will be lost to them.

WiseStamp (www.wisestamp.com) is a free app you can use in your email signature to encourage people to connect with you on your various social media sites. It installs on your online email accounts, and you can set it up in one location to work on numerous email accounts so you only have to update one central location. One limitation is that it does not yet send out from Microsoft Outlook email, but keep checking back as this feature is due to be released in 2013. With minimal effort email can be an effective, free marketing and communication tool for your business.

Activity 4.5

- What CRM will you use in your business?

- Why will past customers come back to your business?

- Will you have a customer loyalty or referrals program to encourage repeat business?

Newsletters

A business newsletter is a publication written on a regular basis, typically to your customers and others who are interested in the business. Your newsletter can share information about the business, educate your readers, include frequently asked questions, include staff or product profiles and provide a call to action around promotional activities your business may be offering. Depending on how much content you generate, the newsletter may be distributed on a daily through to an annual basis. You may publish the newsletter in a paper format and mail it to recipients, or leave copies in the reception or other prominent areas.

There is a tendency today to provide newsletters electronically, as this is cheaper, enables quick distribution and offers digital interactive features. If you are distributing your newsletter electronically, you could initially convert a word document to PDF format and distribute it via your email program. However, the number of newsletters you can distribute electronically will be limited by your email provider. If you need a program to convert Word documents to PDF, download CutePDF (www.cutepdf.com), which installs as a printer on your computer. The next solution level is to use a program such as MailChimp (www.mailchimp.com), which has free through to paid solutions that enable you to design, send and track e-newsletter campaigns. They have groovy newsletter templates that you can customise to suit your needs and lots of support videos and notes. The next level up is a program called AWeber (www.aweber.com), which as well as helping you with a newsletter service has an auto responder function so you can follow up with a client regarding a predefined email after a predefined number of days.

Establishing an accurate customer list is an important asset for your business, and a critical part of your marketing efforts. Rather than mess around with PDFs, I would take the time to try a system such as MailChimp, which can effectively make the process easier and help you build your customer list.

Activity 4.6

- Will you prepare a newsletter for your business?
- How often will you send out newsletters?

Competitor profiles

You should have a clear understanding of exactly who your competitors are.

► How many competitors are there?

► What size are they?

► Where are they located?

► What services do they offer?

► What features and benefits do they offer?

You should ascertain whether the market you want to open your business in is already saturated, or whether there are one or two dominant players that would make it difficult to start a business. You need to be able to demonstrate that your business has a point of difference from its competitors, and give a potential customer a clear reason why someone would use your services rather than alternative services.

For example, if you were planning on opening a juice bar, you may look on the various franchise juice bars as competitors. There are many other 'franchise juice bars' in the marketplace. The franchised businesses have restrictions imposed on them, such as limiting the number of staff they may employ, the area in which they can operate and the products they can serve. Some of the franchised businesses have extensive advertising on radio and in the newspaper. The competitive advantages of 'franchise juice bars' are access to mass marketing, a centralised call centre and support from a well-resourced head office.

With this knowledge, you may use fresh, locally sourced ingredients and promote the business at a grassroots level, demonstrating that you have a unique, high-quality product to encourage locals to support a local business, rather than a large, national or multinational business.

Cooperation vs competition

I am not a competitive person by nature, so rather than be competitive in business, I am cooperative. In business circles the term for cooperative competition has been coined 'coopetition' or 'coopertition'. As a management accountant, and solo flyer, I am fortunate to keep in close contact with my 'competitors', both locally and nationally. Without them, I wouldn't be able to offer and maintain the service I do.

When weighing up cooperation versus competition, I treat my competitors as my peers. They are a technical resource: they provide support during busy times and back-up for when I go on holiday. Together, my competition and I can raise the profile of our industry. As a colleague once told me, 'If we can't help each other, what's point in being in business?'

Having a good relationship with them means I'm never out of touch. For example, I recently had a new scenario to resolve, and I called on my colleagues for their learned advice. I also send business their way when appropriate. For example, I may suggest a client deal with a competitor who has more experience in certain areas. If one of my competitors works with a new client introduced to them by me, I can watch and learn in the background, enhancing my own knowledge.

Naturally, there are some competitors I do not share niceties with. You cannot naively believe everyone shares your business integrity. Some operators will ruthlessly copy IP, steal client lists and badmouth your enterprise. If I feel uncomfortable with their modus operandi, or the relationship is weighted in one direction, I keep my distance.

Good, reliable competition is an invaluable resource and gives our customers confidence in the services that we offer. When you are starting your business, take the opportunity to introduce yourself to your local competitors. They may become great allies and they may offer you some welcome overflow opportunities as you start your business.

Offline activities

For a small business, offline promotional activities can be a very expensive means of promoting your start-up business. Many people are advocating moving away from the expense of advertising in its traditional form (for example, telephone books) and looking at more cost-effective mechanisms. Depending on your community and connections, you may consider letterbox drops, sponsoring local schools or charities, advertising in catalogues or **billboard advertising**. However, offline methods can be expensive and depending on the nature of your business you are likely to get more bangs for your buck with online marketing.

Nevertheless, there are a couple of minimal-outlay offline methods worth exploring: networking and word-of-mouth marketing.

Networking

To me, 'networking' seems a bit of a slimy term. I am aghast at the thought of attending an event promoted as 'networking'. However, many of my friends call me a networking queen, which is a crown I wear uneasily. It seems that I have a genuine interest in people — not necessarily people who are going to provide a benefit for me, just people in general. I like to find out about them. I will even go so far as to jot down notes, and if an opportunity arises in the future, I will touch base with them. To me networking is about building contacts and rapport in a social environment.

What are the benefits of networking for your business? Networking can open doors for your business and enable you to share knowledge with other businesses. The businesses may potentially mutually benefit from future opportunities.

There are different types of networking events. As a business if you are going to attend a networking event, choose wisely as they can be time-consuming and take you away from your business. There are industry specific networking events. I run a monthly networking event for an accounting group. The accountants are unlikely to meet new clients at the meeting. However, they gain knowledge, support contacts and tips about improving their business. There are also general networking events, where you may be able to identify a business-to-business opportunity as you are meeting people outside your own industry.

If you are looking for a networking event, you could initially try your local chamber of commerce, which runs both geographical and interest focused chambers. Or you could ask other business owners or your local councillor, or monitor local events and government departments. You could also search topics of interest to you at www.meetup.com.

If you have never been to a networking event before, make sure you have plenty of business cards to hand out and that you are dressed to represent your business's brand. If you are representing a law firm, you would wear a smart suit; if you are representing the local café, your attire may be on the casual side. People believe your delivery over your words, so if you do meet people, show an interest in what they do — don't think it is just about you telling them what you do!

Word-of-mouth marketing

By providing your customers with a memorable experience, they will share stories of their satisfaction about your products and services to other potential users. This is known as word-of-mouth marketing, and it is perceived to be a credible endorsement as the customer's reputation is on the line when they make the recommendation. Your business may encourage word of mouth by offering referral incentives, sharing stories of customer satisfaction in newsletters or simply wowing them by doing something unexpected. Word-of-mouth marketing is low-cost marketing that can be done offline and online.

Online activities

All businesses need a website. I am not even going to debate this issue with you. Even if you do not plan to sell products or services via a website, it will still serve as an electronic brochure for the services that you offer in your business. When people are online searching for a service or product, they have to be able to find your business. There are numerous solutions for creating a website — some relatively cheap, some prohibitively expensive. It is important that you understand the elements of a website so you can gain an appreciation of a successful website.

Website domain names

A domain name is the web address that identifies where the website is. In the section about naming your business I suggested checking to see if a similar domain name was available. Unregistered domain names, as I write, are relatively cheap, and I do not foresee them becoming more expensive in the future. So I suggest you splurge and buy the domain name you want now. You can buy domain names from various companies. Search with Google and you will be bombarded with numerous options, or speak to your IT or web specialist. I purchase my Australian domain names (.com.au) through Lithium Solutions and my international domain names (.com) through BlueHost. If you don't end up needing it you can always let it lapse.

> **Activity 4.8**
>
> What is the registered domain name of your business?

Website content

The actual content of a website is likely to contain written words and pictures. The purpose of having a website is to be found on the internet. When someone uses a search engine provider such as Google, the search engine looks at the content of your website and uses a complicated algorithm to determine where your website is ranked in the search results. To rank higher, you need to understand and implement search engine optimisation (SEO) strategies. Search engine optimisation essentially wants your website to authentically demonstrate what your business delivers. I suggest you speak to an SEO expert about this as it is an evolving science: what worked yesterday may not necessarily work tomorrow.

The website can be a single page or multiple pages. I suggest you look at other websites to see what you like and what you don't like. Then buy a blank art book from the newsagency and roughly outline what you perceive your website to look like. It will be a lot easier to work it out with the website developer if they have a good idea of what you are trying to achieve.

Website hosting providers

Your website needs to be hosted on an internet server provided by a web host. When pictures or content are changed on the website they are uploaded to the host provider.

An easy and cheap place to start a website is through a service such as Wordpress, where you can choose themes and add plugins and features to your website as you develop it. I use Wordpress and like the flexibility it gives me, but I probably waste too much time tinkering with it!

When you get a website developed, make sure you are the owner of the website and have access to all the administrator passwords. Many a business owner has found they actually had to pay every time they wanted a small update undertaken and were locked out from accessing the website themselves. You also need an understanding of how to manage, change or update the website as and when needed. Obviously, for a major overhaul you would use a specialist, but you should know how to undertake a minor tweak.

Social media

Have you ventured into the amazing new world of social media yet? Part of social media is building an army of advocates behind you, your products and services and your business. When someone on Facebook says, 'Where can I buy some fresh garlic on a Saturday morning?' and a friend responds, 'There is a guy who sells massive garlic bulbs at the New Farm Farmers' Market', the farmer has gained business from a word-of-mouth recommendation, even though he may not have a computer!

There is a plethora of social media platforms. As stated on day 2, you should go to a site such as www.knowem.com or www.namechk.com and check if the business name of your choice is available across popular digital and social media platforms. My name, 'Heather Smith', seems to be a popular name so I can never create my social media names in my own name. I have added 'AU' to the end—HeatherSmithAU—to enable me to have consistency across the different social media platforms. In the start-up stage of your business it is critical that you register your business name with the social media platforms that you may use to market your business. Don't go crazy. You are unlikely to need all of them. At the moment I would say the top five social media platforms that need to be part of your business's digital real estate are Facebook, Twitter, LinkedIn, YouTube and Google Plus, so I would at least grab your **vanity ID** there, and anywhere else you think may be useful to your business.

Facebook

Founded in 2004, Facebook is a social networking site with more than 900 million active users. When you set up a business page on Facebook you should opt for a 'fan page' in the settings. This means that people can simply 'Like' your business page, rather than having to wait for you to approve a friendship request. You will need 25 Facebook friends to claim your business's vanity name, so once you have decided on a business name, set it up and persuade at least 25 people to like your page! Your goal should be to have active users.

Twitter

Founded in 2006, Twitter is a free real-time microblogging tool with more than 140 million active users. The 'Twitter handle' is the name of the twitter account. It is preceded by an '@' symbol. A **tweet** is sent from a Twitter handle and is limited to 140 text characters.

I suggest you use either TweetDeck (www.tweetdeck.com) or HootSuite (www.hootesuite.com) for managing your Twitter account. This enables you to create different focus lists and track responses easily. My Twitter account is *selectively* linked to LinkedIn. If I add '#li' to the end of a tweet, it posts to LinkedIn.

LinkedIn

Founded in 2002, LinkedIn's slogan 'Relationships Matter' embodies the reason why it is the number one social media platform for professionals, with more than 150 million active users. It is an online résumé: a platform for demonstrating your expertise, seeking recommendations for the work you have completed and connecting online with long lost colleagues and current acquaintances. It's nothing short of a source of raw possibilities.

The only business email that I receive and, most importantly, that I take the time to read every week, is the LinkedIn Network Updates email. If you're not receiving this email, you need to change your LinkedIn email settings. (Select 'Settings/ Receiving Messages', and at the 'Network Updates' line, choose 'Weekly Digest Email'). This email summarises the major activities of your network over the past week: profile updates, new connections, new posts, new recommendations, and so on. Likewise, using the 'Share an update' feature enables you to stay in front of your network on a weekly basis.

YouTube

Founded in 2005, and now owned by Google, YouTube is a video sharing website. Its slogan is 'Broadcast Yourself' and there are 800 million unique visitors to YouTube each month. It is free to create your own business channel on YouTube (with a vanity URL) and you can generate an extra revenue stream by joining the YouTube Partner Program and monetising your content.

Google Plus

Launched by Google in 2011 with the slogan 'Real-life sharing rethought for the web', Google$^+$ is a social networking site with more than 200 million active users. It enables you to group people into circles of interest and interact with different circles as you wish.

Social media tips and tricks

There are lots of little tricks when it comes to social media that, when used, can make you look like an expert. It is desirable when sharing information across social media to shorten the hyperlink so that the information is easier to read, can be re-shared and also to prevent a long hyperlink being broken or damaged. I use a free tool known as 'bitly' to shorten hyperlinks. You can visit www.bitly.com, sign up for an account, produce hyperlinks with bitly extensions and your bitly account then tracks and analyses how many people you may have reached with your message.

To see an analysis of when and where people clicked through on the shortened link, copy the bitly hyperlink and add a '+' to the end. Then drop it in the browser's web address field.

Of course, you should also consider that shortening a hyperlink may well disguise the website destination and that this could deter some people from using it. So it can be a good idea to customise the shortened URL address so that it is user friendly.

For example, you could change the hyperlink 'oNBvN6' to 'SignUp4Newsletter'. The following hyperlinks both lead to the same website; however, the second one clearly indicates that the site is for signing up to a newsletter. Enter either one in the website address field of your browser window:

▶   www.bit.ly/oNBvN6

▶   www.bit.ly/SignUp4Newsletter.

Now try entering the following hyperlink in the website address field of your browser window: www.bit.ly/oNBvN6+.

'Social media' is the buzz term in activities at the moment and it can be a time-effective tool that enables you to network with clients and colleagues from your desk. It should be part of your overall communication strategy, not a standalone strategy.

Social media activity should be about building authenticity and credibility within the business industry. Don't link all of your accounts and send out a single message across all sites. That is spamming your followers. Keep your content short, sharp and social. Content is king, but it must be relevant, topical, informative and engaging. A good posting is actionable and stimulates discussion with your followers. You also need to be prepared to promptly respond to customers or enquiries on social media, so make sure you monitor your sites regularly.

Activity 4.9

Which social media profiles will you create for your business?

If you want to learn more about social media, take a look at Linda Coles's book *Learn Marketing with Social Media in 7 Days* (published by Wrightbooks, 2011).

Summary of day 4

Developing your business brand, choosing business colours and fonts, designing a logo, ensuring that you have a customer relationship management system in place to capture details of all customers, creating a website, setting up several social media platforms, outlining a newsletter and drafting a marketing calendar will establish a solid foundation for your business's marketing activities. Just take a look at figure 4.2 for a visual representation of all the components of marketing.

Figure 4.2: the plethora of marketing options available

While setting up the technical aspects of marketing, you can also spend some time reflecting on your network—the network that you have been developing in some shape or another since you were in kindergarten. Not only will they become potential customers and ambassadors of your product, they will also become resources. If you are having trouble solving a problem, you can look to your network for solutions. If your taps are leaking, you call a plumber. But if you come across something in your business you are unsure of, your network and your mentors may be able to share the conversation and shed some light on how to deal with the problem. On day 7 I will discuss where you will find your first client or customer; however, it is important that you are thinking about who will buy from you throughout the seven-day process.

With your draft marketing calendar in place, we are ready to start considering another important aspect of the business: day 5, finances.

Day 5

Finances

Key areas we will cover on day 5:

▶ financing your business

▶ establishing accounting procedures

▶ developing collection policies

▶ analysing financial reports

▶ designing business invoices

▶ budgeting and benchmarking

▶ identifying key performance indicators

▶ maximising income and minimising expenditure.

It is important to understand and plan for the financial side of the business. Many business owners are primarily focused on tax obligations; however, accurate financial reports are useful resources for decision making. You cannot run a business by monitoring your bank statements and assuming a positive balance means the business is in a healthy position and everything is okay. As a business owner you need to look at the business's financial reports on a regular basis to assist you in understanding the performance of the business, and to determine what you can do to achieve your goals and move the business in the direction you want.

Financing your business

Starting your own business may require funding of some sort. It may involve business expenditure, or simply funding the time you dedicate to developing the business. Have you determined where you will find this money? Seed funding can come in many forms: you may have a redundancy payout or be eligible for a bank loan. It could also come from a government grant, an entrepreneurial grant, a business competition, family, friends or personal funds.

You may have heard of companies receiving mind-blowingly large injections of funds. They typically source these funds from venture-capitalists or angel investors. So who are these people? They are usually very savvy business people who assist people with the start-up phase of their business. A venture capitalist uses pooled funding, while an angel investor invests personal money in start-up ventures, typically in exchange for equity. Pop singer Justin Timberlake invested in the social networking site MySpace; this is an example of angel investment.

In reality it is quite rare for an Australian business to source funding through these means while they are still based in Australia. To improve your chances you should travel to Silicon Valley in the United States. Silicon Valley is the epicentre of entrepreneurialism. It has the infrastructure, resources and expertise to be an incubator for start-up companies and is the ultimate incubator experience for innovative start-up companies who shine in the competitive landscape. If this interests you, you will need to have an awesome pitch, a business plan, a financial forecast and demonstrated evidence that the business idea has merit. You will then need to have lots of meetings in coffee shops, and work every angle to wrangle an elusive meeting with a venture capitalist or an angel investor.

There are also some Australian-based organisations who invest in start-ups; for example:

- ▶ Microsoft BizSpark (www.microsoft.com/bizspark/default .aspx)—start-ups in the software cloud space

- ▶ AngelCube (www.angelcube.com)—mentorship, seed capital, connections and opportunities for Australian web start-ups

- ▶ Startmate (www.startmate.com.au)—a group of start-up executives offering mentorship and **seed financing** to technical founders creating global internet start-ups from Australia.

Crowdsourcing capital is an emerging method of raising start-up funds. There are many websites, such as Indiegogo (www.indiegogo.com), where you can pitch your business plan to the market. If investors are inspired, they can invest microsums of money and in return your business may issue a gift or a perk for the investment or donation.

If you seek external funding, the lender will want to see the financial projections of the business, including any contracts or commitments that you may have secured. If you do source funding in the early days, ensure you understand what the funding is committing the business to both in terms of payment, interest payable, obligations and ownership.

Activity 5.1

- What funds do you need to invest into your business before you can start trading?

- What personal funds do you estimate you will require for the first year of your business?

Banking and merchant facilities

As a small business it is essential that you develop a good working relationship with your bank. Do they understand your business? Are they a small-business speciality bank? Do they offer a good deal when it comes to merchant fees, overdraft facilities, interest-bearing accounts and business loans? The rates and services offered will differ among banks and you don't want to be losing your hard-earned money on financing charges!

You may be able to access a range of useful small-business products via your bank: internet and telephone banking, coin swap, lending, vehicle and equipment finance, access to a small-business banker, credit or debit card and EFTPOS. These can be accessed in store, on the road, via your website or over the telephone.

When it comes to banking, you need to set up stand-alone, dedicated business accounts, depending on your business needs—for example, PayPal and credit card accounts. You should try to avoid paying for personal expenses through the business so that there is some certainty that all transactions on the statements are business related. Business-only bank debit and credit card accounts make reconciliations and preparing financial accounts simple. Frankly, at this stage I whisper to all my clients, I don't even care if the accounts are proper business bank accounts—which typically cost more than a personal account—just ensure they are only used for the business.

I would also suggest trying to keep life simple by setting the business up with a single high-street bank. Communications and negotiations can be more contained if you are with a single bank, and you may have more leverage with them if they see you are a loyal customer. (Of course, interest rates at other banks may be more attractive for a term deposit, and you will need to weigh up the financial benefit versus the extra administrative burden.)

Also, when you set up your bank accounts, opt for monthly statements that are delivered to you as close to the end of the month as possible (for manual reconciliation purposes). It is optimal to get clients to directly pay into your business bank account. Another idea that may suit your business is to set up merchant facilities if you want to receive credit card payments. There are a number of options available: you can record the details and process payments via PayPal or merchant facilities, or you can rent an EFTPOS machine and receive payments immediately. You may want to on-charge the merchant fees—which are typically a percentage of the purchase—to the customer.

Your business may receive payments by cash. There is a cost associated with receiving cash: it takes time to process, it needs to be physically banked and it is an easy target for opportunistic thieves. It is also tempting when receiving cash to use it to pay bills, which adds complexity, and sometimes errors, to the bookkeeping process. In addition, productivity lost over time due to daily banking can be considerable.

In any case, it's advisable to make it easy for customers to buy from your business. This may involve giving them a variety of payment options.

Business tax obligations

As an Australian business, if you earn money you will be subject to Australian taxation laws (www.ato.gov.au). The laws and regulations governing this area are quite complicated and subject to change. It is unlikely that you will be abreast of all taxation issues; however, you should have a general understanding of how taxation works in Australia to assist you in managing your business's financial situation. Tax can be a significant expense of your business and, as with any expense, you do have some options regarding how you manage it. Taxation law is vast and you should seek the advice of a small business taxation expert.

One of the first financial decisions to be made when starting a new business is whether you should register for the goods and services tax (GST). GST is a tax on the supply of most goods and services consumed in Australia. It is currently 10 per cent. As a business, registering for the GST means you collect GST on applicable sales, pay GST on applicable purchases and remit the difference to the Australian Taxation Office.

Currently, it's mandatory to register for the GST if you expect your annual turnover to be $75 000 or more. Your 'GST turnover' is defined by the ATO as your gross business income — not your profit — *excluding*:

► any GST you included in sales to your customers

► sales that are not for payment and are not taxable (for example, some sales to associates)

► sales not connected with an enterprise you carry on

► input taxed sales you make

► sales not connected with Australia.

However, if your turnover is likely to be less than $75000, registering for the GST is optional. When deciding whether or not to charge the GST, you should consider the cash flow and administrative implications.

If you're forecasting a turnover below the $75000 threshold, not registering for GST means your selling prices will effectively be 10 per cent cheaper than those of your GST-registered competitors. Or you could charge the same price as your competitors and enjoy a healthier profit margin. On the other hand, you won't be able to claim back the GST on your expenses or on any goods you purchase for sale.

On the negative side, GST registration means additional administration work and reporting to the ATO, typically on a quarterly basis. However, being forced to maintain your financial records in a timely manner will provide valuable insights that assist in the management of the business, so the administration involved in completing your business activity statement (BAS) periodically may be a blessing in disguise.

Certain types of businesses would benefit from not registering for the GST. A business with high service-based sales and minimal expenses and capital purchases may benefit from not being registered for the GST (if that option is available to them).

For example, a GST-registered business with an income of $70000 excluding GST, and outgoings of $10000 excluding GST, would be required to remit $6000 of collected GST to the ATO. This would create a negative impact on its cash flow, as well as additional paperwork. On the flip side, if your non-registered business turns over $70000 it's all yours—at least until the time comes to pay your income tax!

As with all tax issues, you'll need to speak to your tax accountant about whether or not you should register for the GST, based on your individual situation. If you begin your business by not registering for the GST and then find you are obliged to register for the GST you will need to add the GST amount (currently 10 per cent) to your prices, which may upset ongoing prices.

Non-registration does highlight the fact that your turnover is below a certain threshold. However, clients normally won't be aware of this until they receive your invoice and even then it may not be immediately obvious to them. Would you hesitate about purchasing from a business that is not registered for the GST?

However, you should also bear in mind that some businesses are wary of buying from those not registered for the GST, perhaps questioning their credibility. This may affect your sales. Furthermore, some businesses prefer to purchase from a GST-registered business just so they can claim back the GST.

If you want to check whether or not a business is registered for the GST visit the Australian Business Register at www.abr .business.gov.au. On the right-hand side of the home page enter the Australian Business Number (ABN) of the business you wish to check and click 'search'. You'll see current details of the business, including the GST registration status.

Activity 5.2

- Will you register for the goods and services tax (GST)?

- On what date will your business be registered for the GST?

Connecting with the ATO

Once your business has received an ABN, you can register to access your online ATO business portal. A portal is defined as a technological doorway that connects two different locations.

A business portal is an online area that enables you to directly communicate with the ATO, and saves you time and money when lodging business activity statements (BAS) and instalment activity statements (IAS). Once you have access to the portal, you will not receive paper copies of activity statements. To set up your portal, visit www.ato.gov.au and on the right-hand side of the home screen you should see the word 'Portals'. Click on 'Portals' and then click on 'Register'.

Some of the ATO technical jargon can be a bit overwhelming but, essentially, in order to set up the portal you will have to download some software (AUSkey) and install it on your computer. When you download your AUSkey software I suggest you keep a copy on a couple of USB sticks so you can access the portal on other computers. If your computer is replaced you will need to ensure the business portal is reinstalled on the replacement computer.

The ATO offers free informative seminars and workshops on bookkeeping and related issues that are specially designed for small business. If you're really keen, you can even follow the ATO on Twitter (@ATO_gov_au). Use the ATO as a resource when you commence your small business.

Choosing accounting software

The best thing you can do for your business financials is to avoid the legendary shoebox, skip the Excel spreadsheet and move straight onto a proper accounting software solution. Producing your BAS, preparing your business accounts for your tax accountant, invoicing and viewing up-to-date financial reports are only a few of the tasks that will be so much easier to perform. Once you're over the initial hurdle of setting up an accounting package you will be surprised at how much easier it is to manage your business accounts. You will look forward to reading your financial reports and using your business insights to make strategic decisions.

Initially you need to decide on an accounting package that suits your business. Identify the features you need from an accounting solution: payroll, inventory, multicurrency, reporting options, simultaneous users, upgrade path, PC or cloud based. Once you scratch the surface you will find there are a lot of options, but knowing what your goals are will narrow down your choice.

There are several popular options available in Australia. The two main ones worth mentioning are MYOB and XERO.

▶ MYOB Australia has a number of different PC and cloud-based options ranging from ones for microbusiness to larger operations. Refer to my book *Learn MYOB in 7 Days* for more information.

▶ XERO is a cloud-based solution that can integrate with other business-management solutions to streamline your processes. I use XERO as my main accounting solution.

With your chosen software, and your draft reporting requirements, you need to ensure your accounting solution is set up properly. Do not feel that you need to do this on your own; there are many accredited software-specific consultants available to help you onsite or virtually. An experienced consultant will be able to set up a typical business in a couple of hours. The hardest part is the set-up stage, so make this as pain free as possible and invest in a consultant to set up the software correctly.

Empower yourself by undertaking some training in how to use the accounting software and how to access and read the financial reports produced. There is a movement in the small business world to outsource your bookkeeping. I suggest you delegate rather than abdicate responsibility for your finances. If you want longevity in the business world, you must take the time to understand your own business finances. I encourage clients to spend some time really understanding how the system works, and then if they still want to outsource the bookkeeping, do. But don't forget to make time to look at the financial reports.

You need to ensure the information is collected in such a way that it can be extracted and reported as required. Committing to a purpose-built accounting solution will give you the ability not only to easily meet your compliance obligations, but also to produce timely, accurate data that will enable you to make insightful management and strategic decisions.

Accounting 'in the clouds'

The leading players in the accounting software market have all recognised that the future of accounting is in the clouds. Globally accessible online accounting software utilising bank feeds, minimising data entry and maximising efficiency has arrived and it is an option I suggest you seriously consider. I talked extensively about the benefits and concerns of cloud computing on day 3. Today, I am going to specifically talk about cloud accounting solutions.

Cloud accounting software packages such as XERO and MYOB are available wherever you have access to the internet. Online accounting packages utilise bank feeds to minimise data entry and processing time. Online accounting products are linked to the business's bank, credit card and PayPal accounts. Transactions that happen within these bank accounts feed directly into the online accounting package, either live or batched overnight depending on the financial institution. Once the transaction has arrived in the accounting software it needs to be coded. However, once a transaction has been coded, future similar entries will typically recognise the coding rules and will be automatically coded. For example, once you have allocated an account and tax code to a bank charge transaction all future bank charges will be coded the same way. Of course, if necessary the memorised coding can be overridden.

Another feature of online software is that the user never has to back up data or worry about upgrading software as this is done automatically. I would, however, suggest that you download your transactional histories on a monthly basis and take responsibility for storing your own data. I believe the mainstream cloud solutions have invested in reliable infrastructure solutions for backing up data. However, history has shown that cloud accounting solutions may without notice shut down access to your data for a limited period of time.

If you use internet banking you should feel comfortable using online accounting solutions. They will typically offer the same sort of security as internet banking. Like your bank password, you need to be sensible about keeping your online accounting solution access password secure. But the data itself is backed up online offsite and this in itself is probably more secure and reliable than many businesses' current back-up solutions.

Understanding financial reports

There are a number of financial reports you should prepare for monitoring the performance of your business.

Profit and loss

The profit and loss report is a popular report because it (hopefully) shows the business's profit over a period of time and is a figure most people can grasp. Simply put, it is your business income less your business expenditure. When you look at a profit and loss report there are actually three levels of 'profit': gross, operating and net. Figure 5.1 describes each of these.

Figure 5.1: the three levels of profit — gross profit, operating profit and net profit

Profit & Loss Statement	
Business Income **less Cost of Goods Sold** **= Gross Profit**	The **Gross Profit** represents the profit from actually selling a product or service. If you run a service-based business, the related staff costs would be included in Cost of Goods Sold.
Less Operating Expenses **= Operating Profit**	The **Operating Profit** is the Gross Profit less the Operating Expenses of the business (the general expenses required to run the business such as telephone expenditure). If you want to sell your business, you would show prospective buyers the Operating Profit line of the business.
Add Other Income **Less Other Expenses** **= Net Profit**	Operating Profit less non–business-related income and expenses that may be legitimately run through the business equals **Net Profit**. Other Income and Other Expenses are segregated, so that they do not confuse the Operating Profit, the profit generated from running the business. Examples of Other Income and Other Expenses may include financing interest or home office expenses. If the business was sold they would not go with the business.

Balance sheet

The balance sheet is like a photograph in time of the net worth of the business. It is represented by assets less liabilities, which equals the equity of the business. The equity includes the financial year-to-date profit of the business on an accruals basis. By understanding your reports you should be able to establish a chart of accounts that suits your business and provides you with meaningful, useful information.

Accounts receivable report

The accounts receivable report details all money owed to the business. You want to ensure these are kept to a minimum and that all outstanding debts are followed up in a timely manner.

Accounts payable report

The accounts payable report details all money the business owes. You want to ensure that you do not allow payables to go neglected and that you have the cash flow to cover these debts. If you neglect to pay your debts, you may find it difficult to secure future supplies.

Job report

A job report monitors the profit and loss of a particular project or activity of the business. This will give you a better picture of how profitable individual projects are.

Accounts receivable

In the start-up phase of your business, you need to design an invoice, decide on credit terms that you will offer clients, establish procedures for chasing outstanding debts and determine strategies for maximising your income.

You need to set up efficient systems for chasing receivables.

I know a very skilled and experienced craftsman who runs a business, but he struggles to collect outstanding payments. Rather than focus on debt collecting, which is what he needs to do, he focuses on undertaking additional work for the client, so they owe him even more money. He could learn to manage his cash flow, but he is so focused on delivering projects he ignores this side of his operations to the detriment of the whole business.

You need to establish a consistent procedure for collecting debts. If you offer clients or customers payment terms — for example, 'Payment is due in 7 days' — you are effectively loaning them money. Can you avoid this and get payment upfront? If not, make sure the client or customer clearly knows how they need to pay you by way of a well-designed invoice. Keep the communication channels open, make sure the debtor has received the invoice and speak with them if payment runs late.

Business invoices

After years of working in management accounts, I find that the same invoicing errors keep cropping up. There is no approved standard for the format of business invoices. However, an invoice contains a lot of important information that should be presented in a clear and legible manner. You want to design a business invoice that includes all the correct information and helps you get paid on time. You may initially create your invoices in a Word template, but I would encourage you to use the invoicing system within your accounting system.

There are some essential pieces of information that should be on your invoice.

▶ *Business name.* Some businesses have the misconception that an invoice is a promotional tool with logos, brand names and fancy interlocking letters, all of which cloud the purpose of the invoice. While branding is important, it's worth remembering KISS — Keep It Simple Stupid! The invoice is not an advertising document; it needs to convey the name of your business and who payment should be made to in a straightforward way. If you want to promote your business, keep the promotion clearly separate from the invoice's purpose.

▶ *Business address.* Ensure the address where any correspondence should be mailed to is clear and legible. Pay close attention if your logo incorporates the address: check that it is readable when printed in black and white.

▶ *Telephone number.* There should be a phone number on the business invoice that your customer can call for assistance with any accounts queries.

▶ *Purchase order number.* The purchase order number should be clearly stated. It is your record that the customer has initiated and authorised the expenditure in question. You can therefore assist the matching process by highlighting the purchase order number. If you don't use a formal purchase order system, I suggest you use the surname, in CAPITALS, of the person at the company who authorised the payment.

▶ *Invoice number.* The invoice number should be unique because it is used as a control feature on many accounting packages. If you accidentally invoice a purchaser using an existing invoice number, even if the date and amount are different, payment could be refused. You may choose to sequentially number invoices (1, 2, 3…) or make them mnemonic (OCT1, OCT2, OCT3). To give the impression that your business is established, you may start invoicing at a number higher than 1.

▶ *Layout of invoice.* There should be enough blank space on an invoice to allow for additional information to be added. The receiver's accounts payable department may choose to add a date stamp, authorising signature and account allocation.

▶ *Size of paper.* In Australia, our offices are set up to match the A4 sheet size and if you choose something outside of this norm, locating and filing the invoice will be more cumbersome for the companies you are doing business with. Small invoices do get lost and a lost invoice can easily delay payment.

▶ *Type of paper.* If you are mailing a business invoice, I would encourage the use of distinctive coloured or textured paper so that it's easy to find your business's invoice among a pile of bills to be paid.

▶ *Delivery of invoices.* Email is a legal and environmentally acceptable way of sending invoices and emailing an invoice ensures quick delivery.

▶ *Payment details.* Make it easy for companies to pay you, offer them a variety of alternatives and all the payment details they'll need. If they were to make a payment via cheque or postal order, they will need the account name, number and address details. If they are to pay directly into your bank account, they will require your account name, BSB number and account number.

▶ *Taxation requirements.* If you are registered for the GST, your invoice needs to clearly state 'Tax Invoice' and identify the GST component of the invoice. If you are not registered for the GST, you cannot include any references to 'Tax' or GST on the invoice. When it comes to invoices, this is probably the number one mistake I see: invoices claiming a GST even though they are not registered for the GST.

▶ *Australian Business Number.* You need to state the business's ABN and if the purchase is more than $1000, include the supplier's ABN. I also encourage my clients to check the

ABN validity of all new suppliers at www.abr.business
.gov.au to ensure that they are actually registered for the
GST and entitled to claim GST from you. You don't want
to pay 10 per cent GST if you don't have to.

Once you have developed your invoice, try this test. Within
three seconds, circle the following information on your business invoice:

▶ the invoice number

▶ the due date

▶ the total amount due.

If you failed at this task you should review the invoice's
format to ensure payment will be made promptly. I suggest
you refer to the easy-to-read ATO publication titled 'How to
set out tax invoices and invoices (NAT 11675)' to ensure you
are compliant.

Maximising income

If you have not been provided with recommended retail prices
for your product, you will need to determine a selling price
for the products you offer. You also need to have a clear idea
of the full cost of the product to you, so you can ensure you
price for profit. The market research you did on day 1 may
assist you in determining the price your market will pay for
your product. There are numerous pricing strategies that you
can utilise—from cost-plus pricing to premium pricing and
psychological pricing—and you may find you need to test a
few out to see what results in a suitable profit.

Activity 5.3

- How will you price the products or services you have on offer?

- How will your prices compare with your competition's?

Product or service	Our price	Competitor price (range)

Accounts payable

I have heard so many excuses as to why an invoice has not been paid on time. As I listen on the other end of the phone, or read as the recipient of an email, I roll my eyes and wonder does the customer truly expect me to believe these feeble excuses?

Some of the ways customers have tried to avoid paying invoices include pretending they've paid the invoice, pretending they never received the invoice and telling me that the person who needs to approve the invoice is away. Maybe you can use these when you next need to avoid paying those annoying invoices! Of course, these ideas are totally unhelpful and written tongue-in-cheek. Avoiding paying your invoices is not much fun for either party. If you do find yourself struggling to pay your debts, I truly believe you should be upfront and honest with the supplier. Communicate with them: perhaps you can renegotiate payment terms, work out a payment plan or provide contra goods or services? Monitor your cash flow and don't overextend yourself; don't make agreements to purchase goods or services you cannot pay for. Don't be the customer who feeds your invoices to the dog.

Minimising expenditure

Minimising expenditure is a critical component of business survival and cash flow. Follow these practical expense management guidelines to help keep your business expenses under control.

▶ *Plan your expenditure.* When considering any business expenditure, question whether it's really necessary, and if so, whether you need it now. Will you utilise the item or service as soon as it's purchased, or can the expenditure be delayed?

This is an example of why it's useful to have a budget in place for your business. If you've already determined your spending limits for the period you are in a better position to decide whether a particular expense is feasible.

▶ *Assess your return on investment (ROI).* What is the ROI of the expenditure? What will it return to the business over a period of time — say, a year? Will expenditure lead to income generation? Will it have a resale value? Do you really understand what it will contribute to the business?

With the answers to all these questions in mind, is it worth the money?

▶ *Compare prices.* If you decide to go ahead with the expenditure, shop around, compare prices, seek quotes, watch the sales, use vouchers and always try to negotiate a better price.

▶ *Be accountable.* Are you being held accountable for your business spending? Discussing business expenditure with your partner, accountant, business coach or advisory board on a regular basis can be a valuable business growth strategy, and may help you identify new money saving tips.

▶ *Think outside the box.* Is there a way you can have the product or service you want without spending the money? Are there borrowing, co-sharing or renting options available?

▶ *Appreciate replacement costs.* Expenditure on replacement items may be avoided if they are treated with respect and serviced in accordance with the manufacturer's guidelines. One restaurant I worked with on the Gold Coast had a collage of plates and glasses on their wall with the cost underneath. Breaking a glass is not just a broken glass; it is an additional five dollars in expenses to the business. Helping your staff understand this may encourage the staff to be more careful when dealing with your business's property.

Like one of my clever clients, you may find it fun to turn money saving into a game, competing against yourself to spend less and less with every passing month. Another client rents an office for his business, and then sublets the space he doesn't need at a rate that more than covers his own rent.

It may seem exhausting and onerous to apply these expense management guidelines to every purchase. You need to undertake a cost versus benefit analysis when reviewing expenses; that is, if savings are considerable then it is worth the time you spend reviewing the expenditure. It is essential to understand that unnecessary expenditure could lead to cash flow problems. I have firsthand experience of watching businesses misguidedly outlay huge expenses early in their operation, only to teeter on the brink of collapse for months or years afterwards. Spending money wisely will enhance the stability and longevity of your business.

> ## Activity 5.4
> Can you highlight ways of reducing expenses in the business?

Bookkeeping procedures

It is important that you take the time to set up a filing system for securely storing your financial documents. Create folders entitled 'Data entry', 'To be paid', and 'To be filed or scanned', and I recommend filing your paperwork in date order in a lever arch file, or if you opt for a paperless office, scan and name the documents, and name the file directories appropriately.

Exclusively use a *red* pen to neatly make notations on any paperwork pertaining to expenses, such as the reason for the expense, the client it relates to, the amount and date of the payment and, if relevant, whether it is to be a split allocation.

Ask your tax accountant what documents they will require the business to supply at the end of the year, and if practical, maintain a separate file for the end of financial year paperwork (for example, bank statements, leases and fixed asset purchases). It may seem a long way off now, but the simple task of preparing a file for the anticipated paperwork will save you a lot of headaches at the end of the financial year.

There are many repetitive procedures within the accounts department and it is useful to ensure all aspects of the work are completed to checklists. I've created some checklist templates to get you started, which you're welcome to download from my website. Visit www.HeatherSmithSmallBusiness.com.

For more in-depth information about accounting and bookkeeping aspects of your business refer to the books *Learn Bookkeeping in 7 Days* and *Learn Small Business Accounting in 7 Days* (published by Wrightbooks in 2010 and 2011, respectively).

Budgets and forecasts

An annual budget is a financial listing of all planned business income and expenses over a period of time. Preparing a budget forces you to consider the financial spending of the business. There are a number of benefits of preparing a budget, including the following:

▶ will help you set motivational goals for achieving income

▶ can help plan for future expenditure and ensure you are not overstretching the business finances

▶ can help evaluate the performance of the business

▶ will help you appreciate your financial situation, and encourage responsible spending

▶ can be an early warning signal of potential financial problems

▶ is necessary if your business needs to borrow money as lenders will want to look at a prepared budget

▶ will assist you in learning about your business and aid you in preparing accurate forecasts of future financial performance.

Typically budgets are broken into monthly periods stretching from 12 to 36 months, with 'Income' and 'Expenses' listed as line items. Hopefully you have been thinking about your business budget already. Once you have committed to your annual budget, you may re-forecast against it during the year.

You can prepare a budget in your accounting software or on a spreadsheet. Enter the monthly periods across the top of the columns, and enter the income and expenditure in the rows beneath.

In the start-up phase of your business it may be difficult to gather all the information you need to prepare a budget so treat it as a work in progress: as you learn about your business's needs—including legal fees and advertising—enter each expense or income. Anticipate the demand for your product or service and take note of all aspects of the expenses: the amount, the regularity and when you will be required to pay it. A budget should also include detailed assumptions; for example, lease expenses are fixed for five years, an additional full-time employee will be employed every six months, and so on. As you discover the real amounts, these figures can be updated.

An example of a budget spreadsheet is shown in figure 5.2. If, for instance, you know you are committed to a regular telephone bill you can include that amount in the budget.

Figure 5.2: a sample budget spreadsheet

	Jan	Feb	Mar	Apr	May	Jun	Jul	Aug	Sep	Oct	Nov	Dec
Income												
Expenses												
Telephone	$60	$60	$60	$60	$60	$60	$60	$60	$60	$60	$60	$60
Net												

If putting together a complete budget for your business is too daunting, at least formulate a plan and time frame for expenditure on the major areas of your business.

Inventory management

Will your business be dealing with inventory? Will you have stock that you need to invest in, store securely, display to customers and ultimately sell?

Investing in stock can be a considerable cash drain on the business. In terms of stocking your shelves with the products you are planning to sell, bare white shelves with minimal products is chic. However, customers are reluctant to 'take the last piece of cake off the plate'. Buying psychology suggests customers want to shop when there are more rather than fewer products available, so you will need to invest in inventory to keep your shelves stocked.

You may find yourself in a continual balancing act of trying to order just the right amount of stock. There would be no stocktake sales if stock purchasers were able to match stock requirements to customer needs.

A stocktake provides the business with an accurate idea of the number of stock items that the business owns. This enables the accountant to reconcile physical stock to the inventory records, highlights variances, and perhaps identifies issues with stock management and control. It is important to have systems in place to monitor stock movement.

If you have accurate knowledge about stock movement and stock on hand, you can deal with theft, slow-moving items, damaged stock, technology obsolescence and warehouse processes and you can make informed decisions about your inventory.

Financial benchmarks

Benchmarks are financial tools you can use to evaluate the performance of your business in relation to **best practice** within your industry. In simple terms they will compare your numbers with those of similar businesses.

Benchmarks can help you develop strategies for improvement. Comparing business data to benchmarks may draw attention to areas of your business that need to be examined, and those that are performing above standard and can potentially be exploited. Benchmarks can also assist in preparing budgets.

Many organisations that collect data provide financial benchmarking information for free, and include government organisations, banks, industry associations, franchise groups and universities.

The ATO provides small business benchmarks for more than 100 industries (see www.ato.gov.au/businessbenchmarks). If your business is performing outside of these benchmarks you may be waving a red flag for a tax audit. For example, if your business income is low in relation to other businesses in the industry you may need to review the recording of cash income and bookkeeping practices and make sure that you're fulfilling your tax compliance obligations.

Of course, it's important to remember that not all businesses are the same. For financial benchmarking to be used effectively, the comparative data needs to be from similar businesses of a similar size. Other variations may distort comparisons within industries too. For example, your individual location may result in your business having higher rent and labour costs than your competitors.

What are some examples of financial benchmarking? Take a look at the performance benchmarks provided by newsagents at www.ato.gov.au/businessbenchmarks. Here you'll see a clear explanation of how the ATO defines a newsagency, and what business is included and excluded. In this particular example three ratios are provided across three annual turnover ranges:

▶ cost of goods sold as a ratio of turnover

▶ labour as a ratio of turnover

▶ rent as a ratio of turnover.

Each of the three ratios examines the relationship between the business turnover and a key business expense: cost of goods, labour or expenses.

This exercise underlines why it's important to measure what's important to your business in order to have the data available for comparison.

So, how do you use this information?

If the benchmarks identify your rent expense as being considerably higher than industry norms, you may want to try to renegotiate your rent with your landlord, or look at downsizing or changing location.

Likewise, if your cost of goods or labour is high you may choose to review your staffing or spending habits or focus on introducing efficiencies.

On the flip side, your benchmarks may show that you need to work harder to get sales or that you need to raise your prices.

Summary of day 5

Numbers are important: they need to be correct and available on a timely basis. You need to understand what your tax obligations are and plan for your expenditure. You may want to outsource your bookkeeping tasks, but you cannot abdicate responsibility of your tax or financial situation. Utilise experts to assist you in setting up this aspect of your business, and regularly monitor your cash position while maximising your income and minimising your expenditure. Don't let the numbers bog you down: try to measure what you need to know about your business in order to manage it.

On day 6 we will talk about one of the business's most important assets and most significant expenses: staff.

Day 6

People power

Key areas we will cover on day 6:

▶ creating an organisation chart

▶ determining your personnel requirements

▶ the implications of employing personnel

▶ recruiting staff

▶ contracting and outsourcing personnel.

If you want to work *on* your business rather than *in* your business, you may have to engage people to do the work for you. This can be done by employing staff, or by contracting or outsourcing personnel.

To do this you will need to relinquish some control while having procedures and processes in place. Employment is a regulated area and there are numerous things to consider. Once the arduous task of recruiting, interviewing and hiring has been completed, it is time for the business to navigate its way through the array of administrative requirements. Then there are the expenses. When you start a business it is unlikely that you will take a proper wage, but your staff will expect to be paid.

People can be one of the greatest assets of a business, while also being a considerable expense. Whether you need to engage staff, engage contractors or outsource work, it is critical for your business's success to surround yourself with the right people — people who are committed and who share your vision — but you need to mix it up. We both know you are awesome but you don't want to fill your organisation with replicas of you. You need different sorts of people in your business: those who are creative and those who are structured. You need to employ people younger than you, older than you and wiser than you. You need to understand that people are different from you, and that they are different from each other. Some may require a lot of direction when they start working with you; others may hit the ground running. Moving from a solo operation will be a major milestone for your business.

Creating an organisation chart

An organisation chart is a graphical means of outlining the management and staffing structure of a business: who reports to whom and which personnel operate on a similar level of authority. You need to make an assessment of the skills, qualifications and other requirements your business operation needs. An organisation chart will also help staff understand where they fit into the organisation.

You can create an organisation chart in Microsoft Office Excel, PowerPoint or Word, or you can try software such as OrgPlus at www.getorgplus.com.au. (There are a few **open source** free options on the market, but maintaining privacy over business data may make these unsuitable options.) If, for example, you wanted to open a coffee shop, you would identify the roles that need to be filled and map them to the organisation chart, as you can see in figure 6.1.

Figure 6.1: identifying roles to be filled

Roles to be filled at a coffee shop: baristas, cash-register operators, cleaners, managers, marketing people, accountant, bookkeeper, purchaser, health and safety officer (and the list goes on).

Obviously, a typical coffee shop cannot afford to employ full-time staff to undertake only one role each. Staff will be expected to undertake several roles: make coffee, operate the cash register, deal with suppliers and clean up. So, the job descriptions will incorporate a variety of roles. A simple organisation chart could look like figure 6.2.

Figure 6.2: a business organisation chart

An organisation chart will assist you in understanding the skills and staff your business requires.

Activity 6.1

Outline the anticipated organisation chart for your business.

Determining your personnel requirements

Before you engage someone to work for your business, establish what work needs to be done and the goals you want to achieve. Putting together a business procedure manual, developing an organisation chart, defining job descriptions and understanding what skills and experiences the business requires may help you in this process.

I once met a lady who ran a consulting business. She told me she planned to employ someone once she had written down the procedures for dealing with every single situation that the person might encounter. Her plan was noble, yet I think somewhat flawed. She had already spent three years developing this all-encompassing business handbook, and I got the impression that it would never be finished. Don't let analysis paralysis stifle your business. As well as employment obligations, there are many other aspects that you should be considering, but these may not fully come to light until you dip your toe in the water and engage someone, in whatever capacity, to do work for the business.

If you want someone to work for your business, a common option is to employ them. You can employ people on a casual, part-time, permanent part-time or full-time basis. Each type of employment has different obligations. Table 6.1 outlines these obligations.

Table 6.1: compliance requirements for different employment statuses

Status	Obligations
Casual	Paid on an hourly basis No accrual of leave entitlements Eligible for superannuation
Part-time	Paid on an hourly basis No accrual of leave entitlements Eligible for superannuation
Permanent part-time	Paid on an hourly basis Accrual of leave entitlements (annual, personal and long-service leave) Eligible for superannuation and redundancy
Full-time	Paid a set wage for the year, allocated according to the payment period. May be entitled to overtime payment. Accrual of leave entitlements (annual, personal and long-service leave) Eligible for superannuation and redundancy The hourly rate will typically be below the rate for a casual employee or contractor because the other options do not attract entitlements.

Employing personnel

Engaging workers is a regulation minefield, so if you plan to grow your business you need to understand what your obligations are.

Record keeping and privacy

In accordance with privacy laws, many documents that you maintain about your staff must be kept in a secure area—for example, locked drawers or password protected for between five and seven years, depending on the information. Refer to www.business.qld.gov.au/business/starting/starting-a-business/record-keeping-business/basic-record-keeping-requirements and www.privacy.gov.au for further information about the business obligations and documents that must be kept.

Activity 6.2

Where will you securely store personnel data?

Modern awards

Here in Australia we have a system known as modern awards, which covers most workplaces. It sets out the minimum criteria for employees and employers in Australia.

When it comes to determining pay rates you can contact the Fair Work Infoline (13 13 94 or www.fairwork.gov.au) or your industry body, which may be able to give you some guidance. There are numerous pay awards that may seem appropriate but may not exactly suit your employees. It is essential that you select the correct pay awards for your staff.

If the position falls outside the modern awards system, at a minimum the national employment standards apply. To determine a fair salary you can try the PayCheck link on the www.fairwork.gov.au website or you can benchmark against salary surveys conducted by leading recruiting organisations. They are available on their websites for free and will assist you in determining a fair market rate. Remember that it is easy to give someone a pay rise, but not so easy to reduce someone's pay. Start as low as possible without putting off quality talent.

Activity 6.3

Do you know which pay awards will be appropriate for your staff?

Codes of practice

You will need to establish codes of practice for harassment, discrimination and bullying behaviour within your business. Your industry association may be able to give you generic codes that you can use, or you can adapt ones sourced from the internet. Alternatively you could ask your lawyer to draft one for the business (expensive) or ask if they can provide a standard template for a start-up business (cheap) that you can then adapt to your circumstances.

Visa status

To work in Australia, you have to be an Australian citizen or hold a work visa. It is a criminal offence to employ someone who is not eligible to work in Australia. If a new employee declares they are not an Australian citizen, you can check the status of their visa online on the Department of Immigration and Citizenship website. For those readers outside Australia, check your government's own visa work regulations.

Tax file numbers

The business is responsible for withholding pay as you go (PAYG) tax from employees. To determine what tax rate is applicable to an employee, you need to provide the new employee with a Tax File Number Declaration Form. A paper copy has to be completed and can be obtained from the Australian Tax Office (www.ato.gov.au/content/6360.htm) or selected newsagencies. If the form is not returned within 14 days, the business is required to withhold 46.5 per cent of any payment—a nice incentive for the payee to return a completed form promptly! The form can be submitted online via SBR compliant software, or you can mail it.

Tax rate tables

Tax rate tables, used to calculate the PAYG withholding tax, are issued by the ATO for each financial year. The ATO sends out paper copies, there is a tax calculator on the ATO website and the tax tables are incorporated into the latest release of accounting payroll software.

Superannuation

All eligible employees are entitled to superannuation guarantee (SG) contributions from their employer if they are paid in excess of $450 in a month. The current super guarantee contribution is 9 per cent of the standard hours of work, which is known as **ordinary times earnings**. The employee is not paid superannuation on income such as overtime, non–work related bonuses or holiday leave loading. Eligible employees are typically aged between 18 and 69 years. If the employee is under 18 years of age they need to work 30 hours per week to be entitled to super contributions. The employment status is irrelevant—the employee can be working full-time, part-time, casually or can be a temporary resident of Australia—they are still entitled to super guarantee contributions from their employer.

If your business pays a contractor who has an ABN and invoices the business, they may still be considered an employee for super purposes. Your business may be obliged to pay the contractor super guarantee contributions. So even if the contractor agrees with the business it doesn't have to pay them super, you may nonetheless be obliged to pay it. If you opt not to pay because as a business you believe the contractor is not entitled to superannuation contributions, I urge you to clarify your decision with your lawyer. I have spoken to a number of lawyers about the situation, and even when contractors worked through their own Pty Ltd business structure, I prudently paid them superannuation on top of their invoices. I could see no way of avoiding it.

If you are dealing with medical 'service providers' rather than contractors, then typically this requirement does not apply. The amount they invoice incorporates super and they are responsible for making their own arrangements.

If you use contractors you need to be very careful about whether you have to pay them superannuation. There is a tool on the ATO website that you can use to determine whether the worker is considered a contractor or an employee. However, I feel the tool has its limitations and through consultative forums have told the ATO this. I believe it can be manipulated to get the result you want. I have talked to two lawyers and asked them to draw up contracts for contractors, and both advised me there was no wording I could use to guarantee I would not have to pay the contractor superannuation. I have spoken to accountants who have clients who are being asked to pay superannuation to their contractors. In addition they have to pay associated fines and interest charges. The fines associated with not paying superannuation are enormous.

In my own business I pay contractors superannuation when their invoice is greater than $450 for the month. I use the same criteria as I would if they were an employee. The thought of superannuation fines terrifies me!

Employers are required to pay superannuation payments on a quarterly basis. This is set out in table 6.2 (overleaf).

Table 6.2: payment dates for employee superannuation

Pay period	Payment due
Quarter 1: July–September	28 October
Quarter 2: October–December	28 January
Quarter 3: January–March	28 April
Quarter 4: April–June	28 July

The employee's payslip will detail their superannuation entitlement for each pay run. Some businesses choose to pay superannuation on a regular basis to enable them to manage their cash flow. However, the actual superannuation payment is only due after the end of the quarter. The super payment must arrive in the employee's superannuation fund by the payment due date, and the business can be fined for late payment. For all four quarters of superannuation payments to be deemed a tax deduction in the financial year in which they were accrued they must be paid by 30 June of that financial year.

Many employees are entitled to select the fund that their superannuation is paid into. When an employee is initially recruited, the employer must issue them with a superannuation choice form, and the new employee needs to sign off that they have received the superannuation choice form. The superannuation choice form can be located on the ATO website at www.ato.gov.au/content/downloads/SPR56761NAT13080.pdf or you can create and print it directly from your MYOB AccountRight software: go to the Setup menu, choose General Payroll Information and click on Print Superannuation Choice Form. The new recruit has 30 days to return the superannuation choice form to the issuer. As some employees may not have a superannuation fund, the business is also required to select a default superannuation fund. If the employee does not return the form within 30 days, their superannuation entitlement can be paid into the business's default superannuation fund. The superannuation payment belongs to the employee, and they can roll over or transfer the money into their own super fund at any time.

For businesses with fewer than 20 employees the Australian Government offers a free superannuation clearing house service. You can find out more about this and register at www.medicareaustralia.gov.au/super/index.jsp. Superannuation contribution payments can be made in one transaction and the superannuation clearing house will prepare the payments to go to the individual superannuation funds. Employees and their selected superannuation fund can be added and removed as required. This reduces the business's administrative burden.

Activity 6.4

Have you selected a default superannuation fund for your business?

Fringe benefits tax

A fringe benefit is a non-salary benefit provided to an employee. Employers are obliged to keep relevant records of any benefits provided to employees so their tax accountant can determine whether there will be a fringe benefit tax (FBT) obligation. Typical fringe benefits include providing a car to an employee who partially uses it for private use or providing a loan to an employee at a low or zero interest rate.

Insurance and WorkCover

Each state has its own WorkCover scheme, a compulsory insurance for workers' compensation. Contact them directly as they have different rules and regulations. Typically the insurance payment is calculated based on an estimate of annual salaries of employed staff and does not include directors' wages.

Queensland WorkCover asks for an estimate of employee wages at the start of the payroll year and then confirms the actual wages at the end of the payroll year, so you are not penalised for overestimating.

Also remember to notify any existing insurance policies of new recruits where relevant.

Occupational health and safety

Occupational health and safety (OH&S) is everyone's responsibility and is applicable to everyone who deals with your business. A safe working environment, first-aid kits, a first-aid officer, clear procedures for reporting OH&S concerns, and a designated fire route and meet-up point are standard OH&S requirements for any business. Other extras such as having plants in the office and healthy food options in the kitchen actively demonstrate an interest in the health and welfare of staff and can boost morale and in turn productivity. Find more information on the government site at australia.gov .au/topics/health-and-safety/occupational-health-and-safety.

Confidentiality agreements

A confidentiality or non-disclosure agreement is a legal document that restricts employees from disclosing intellectual property gained while in employment. This may include restricting the employee from contacting the company's clients, sharing company knowledge with third parties and taking company documents when they leave the business. As a business you need to protect the intellectual property that you develop. I have known start-up businesses where past employees leave, start businesses in competition with their former employer and contact clients they met via the former business. Common sense says this is unfair, but you need to cover all bases and include a confidentiality agreement as part of the employment process.

Personnel specialists

You don't need to go through the staff employment process all on your own. There are specialists you can call on for assistance as you grow and find the need to invest in staff.

▶ A learning and development coordinator can assist with identifying your training needs and implementing development plans for employees.

▶ An industrial relations consultant can assist with all things related to work conditions (such as entitlements and rates of pay) and navigate the complicated minefield that is the modern award system.

▶ A workplace health and safety consultant can assist in ensuring the business adheres to government workplace health and safety regulations.

For a small business a general human resource consultant may be able to help you with all of these requirements and assist with implementing policies and procedures where necessary. You can refer to the Australian Human Resources Institute (www.ahri.com.au) to find a specialist in this area.

Contractors

A contractor or a sub-contractor — or 'subbie', as they are colloquially known — invoices for the hours they have worked or the work they have done. No work, no pay. They may have an ABN and be registered for the GST, and they should have their own insurance. They will not accrue entitlements such as annual or personal leave, unless it is in their contract (but read the section on superannuation on p. 140 for more about this). Their hourly rate is higher than that of employed staff; however, if for example, they are working on a building site and it rains, they don't work and they don't get paid. They generally have expertise in their field or industry and should need minimal guidance.

The contractor will offer their services to several organisations, have some flexibility around when the work will be done and can accept or refuse the work on offer. As you would expect, a contractor is entitled to operate in a safe and healthy workplace that complies with occupational health and safety standards.

Hiring contractors is attractive for a business because they do not have to be concerned with the compliance obligations that come with employing staff. The business does not have to deal with unions, collective bargaining, unfair dismissal, redundancy and other similar costs related to employing staff. However, as you are not committed to a long-term relationship with the person, the contractor may not be available when you need them because they are working elsewhere. You have less control over them and they may work for your competitor. If the contractor creates copyrighted work, they may be considered the owner of this work, unless they have formally agreed to transfer copyright.

While we are discussing the concept of contractors, you may in fact launch your business in the guise of simply being an independent contractor offering services. This is essentially how I started out. I provided training in many different business subjects, including Microsoft Office and MYOB. I developed relationships with a variety of training organisations in Brisbane, let them know what training I could do, and then sent them my calendar of availability. They in turn could book me to run training courses for them. Would this method of securing work suit the sort of business you want to launch?

Outsourcing

Outsourcing involves arranging for external providers to undertake tasks for your business. This is in contrast to contracting, where people are hired on a contractual basis to work. You may be familiar with the concept of outsourcing from media reports; for example, a large business arranges for call centres to operate in a foreign country where labour is cheaper. However, outsourcing is a mechanism that can easily be utilised by a small business.

Today there are a number of websites that facilitate the outsourcing process such as Odesk (www.odesk.com), Elance (www.elance.com) and the Australian-based site Freelancer (www.freelancer.com.au). These types of websites enable small businesses to connect with freelancers or virtual assistants (VAs) who are available for work. In some cases the perception is that the freelancer at the other end of the website is cheap labour; for example, someone from an emerging economy such as India, Sri Lanka or the Philippines. However, through my own experiences I have discovered freelancers at the other end of the website are also stay-at-home mums, retirees earning some extra money or moonlighters who want to do work at home in their own hours. Payment to outsourcing websites can be made by credit card or PayPal and you agree to pay either by the hour or by the completed project.

If you are interested in outsourcing a business task, I suggest you start with a small, non-important task that you can define really well, such as transcribing. You then post detailed requirements of the task on an outsourcing website and freelancers, or in some cases businesses who specialise in the service, will bid to do the task for you. You then have the opportunity to interview them. I suggest you ask specific questions about the task to find out how they respond and if they communicate in a manner you are happy with. Review their bids. Make sure they have some work history and have delivered completed projects. Check that you know exactly what you are committing to. I was interviewing a freelancer about doing some work for me by the hour. I estimated it would take 30 minutes. He estimated it would take 20 hours. If I had committed to an open-ended hourly arrangement, I would have been upset when I got the bill. Communication combined with clear, concise instructions is critical to the success of outsourcing work.

When you hire a freelancer via an online outsourcing website, one of the features many of the sites offer is that screen shots are automatically taken at intervals of the computer monitor as the work is being completed. The freelancer logs into the website at their end, starts the timer to record the work and then screen shots are taken at random intervals. As the hirer you can see if they are daydreaming on Facebook or working on your very important project! Sometimes work does take longer than anticipated, and this feature does assist in building up a level of trust and understanding between the two parties.

Once you find a freelancer who works well with you, you can add them to your team on the outsourcing website and use them to do regular work for you. If you are working with freelancers overseas, one thing you need to be aware of is that while you may establish a relationship with one person, they may be part of an agency. This means that the next time you do work with them, you may be allocated to someone else. Make sure you check as this is not always made clear.

I utilise the services of freelancers based in Australia and overseas. Some tasks, such as making phone calls, are more suited to Australia, while updating my website can be done in Sri Lanka. I like the fact that I can pay people in poorer countries for work, rather than giving them charitable handouts. Not every outsourced job is a success, but payment is usually very low. However, if you are paying a minimal amount to have these tasks done, you can expect hiccups along the way. I am always happy to pay a bonus when the work has been done well.

The recruitment process

Initially you need to develop a job description for a position you are looking to fill. Then you will need to design an advertisement and place it where potential recruits will see it. To assist you, you may work with a recruitment consultant or agency or utilise a recruitment specialist through this process.

Once you have some candidates, provide them with an application form to complete (more on this later). You should then spend time dealing with inquiries, working through applications, shortlisting applicants and preparing for the interview process. The interview can be one on one, a panel interview or a group interview if you are looking for a lot of staff.

After the interview process you may shortlist again and then undertake further assessments of any potential employees to see if they will be a good fit for the organisation. Further assessments may include knowledge and psychometric testing, medical assessments, drug testing and reference checks. In today's age, you will also probably want to Google the applicant, check out their LinkedIn and hope you don't find them on Facebook! During this process, depending on the level of the job position, you may conduct a second and even a third interview.

Once you have selected the ideal candidate, offer them the job, provide them with an employment contract and inform them of the package you are offering. They should then be given time to review and hopefully accept your offer; otherwise you will have to go back to the shortlist.

Job descriptions

A job description is a written outline of the tasks, responsibilities and requirements of a job role. It ensures both the employer and employee understand what is required of the employee within the organisation. A clearly defined job description will assist the employment process as the applicant will understand what the role involves and the employer will be able align the skills of the applicant with the skills required to do the job and assess if they match.

Employment application forms

When a prospective new employee approaches your organisation about a potential job you should use this opportunity to collect as much information as possible from them in the guise of an employment application form. Typically, a new applicant will provide you with a résumé. However, it may be incomplete and you may find it time-consuming to re-order the information into a standardised business format that suits you. So, while you are assessing the applicant's suitability, take the opportunity to see how they complete tasks by getting them to complete an employment application form. You should consider asking for information like that contained in figure 6.3.

Figure 6.3: a sample employment application form

Personal details	Education	Experience
Full name _____ Date of birth _____ Address _____ _____ Tax file number _____ Visa status _____ _____	Details of education, qualifications, certificates undertaken (include time frame) ___ _____ _____ _____	Details of previous employment (include time frame) _____ _____ _____ _____

An employment application form is an example of a standard template that should be included in your business handbook.

Interviewing

Recruitment is the process of selecting, interviewing and employing staff to work for your business. Labour can be a significant expense for a business and recruiting suitable staff can be a costly exercise depending on the expertise and skill levels required. You may turn to a recruitment consultant who can assist with writing job descriptions, advertising for candidates and interviewing applicants.

You may be surprised by how much employees know and don't know. A gifted and highly qualified individual may not understand the basics of addressing a business letter, so you will need to have procedures in place for employees to follow. In the early days you may want to hire people with experience in a similar role. I suggest you consider avoiding hiring family and friends as you will view them through rose-coloured glasses and may not be able to properly assess their abilities.

As mentioned previously, to assist the process you should develop a suitable application form and perhaps a questionnaire about the actual role. The applicant's responses will give you an indication of their knowledge level and their ability to communicate. When some of my clients were looking for a full-time bookkeeper I gave them a questionnaire (to give to the applicants) and supplied them with the answers. Some of the applicants who arrived for an interview refused to do the questionnaire and left! I was shocked, but at least my clients were not wasting time with someone who was not prepared for the challenge of the role.

There are various ways of finding help for your business.

▶ *Join us.* Add a page to your website to inform potential staff about your company, and encourage them to proactively apply online using a contact form. Never put your email address on your website or you will become a target for spam.

▶ *Job networks.* There are websites such as the free government site Australia Job Search (www.jobsearch.gov.au).

▶ *Networking.* You may know someone through your existing social and business networks who would suit the position you are looking to fill.

▶ *Job boards.* Educational institutions such as universities, TAFEs, industry associations and government employment organisations frequently have job boards where you can advertise positions to their members for free. Obviously if you are looking for hospitality staff you should advertise at an institution that runs hospitality courses.

▶ *Advertising.* You can advertise through the local paper or online recruitment sites such as seek (www.seek.com.au) or careerone (www.careerone.com.au). The professional social media site LinkedIn also offers targeted advertising if you're looking for professional staff. When advertising a job, consider where potential employees would look for employment, to optimise your chances of finding the ideal candidate.

▶ *Recruitment companies.* There are specialised businesses that for a fee (and the fee can be quite large) can assist in finding staff for your business. Typically they can assist with the interview stage of the process, which many people find difficult. They may also offer a guarantee if the matching process does not work out within a certain time frame.

The true cost of employing staff

As I have discussed before there are many costs associated with employing someone, and this is something you need to build into your budgeting process. The cost may run up to 100 per cent of the salary as there are the initial costs, ongoing costs and leaving costs over the lifetime of an employee's employment to consider. Figure 6.4 will give you some idea of the costs involved.

Figure 6.4: employment costs that you should consider

Initial costs	Paid advertisements Recruitment
Ongoing costs	Paid entitlements (annual leave, personal leave) SGC contribution Training Perks or bonuses Software licences Workstations Insurance Consumables (business cards, mobile phone) Jury service
Leaving costs	Annual leave Replacement cost Redundancy Lost productivity

Connecting with your employees

There are small ways of making your employees feel comfortable in your business. Feeling appreciated and content in their surroundings will help encourage your staff to perform at a desirable level.

Motivating employees

If you are planning on employing staff at your location you may need to consider a break-away or lunch area that includes coffee- and tea-making facilities as well as a suitably sized fridge for their lunch. If you want to be extravagant you may even invest in an easy-to-use coffee machine. Leaving the office to buy fancy coffee is time consuming and unproductive.

Employee starter packs

To ensure you meet all your employment obligations when a person commences working in your business, issue them with an employee starter pack. You can adapt this pack for contractors.

It should include forms such as the following to be completed and returned to the business:

► an employment contract

► an employee information and contact details form

► a tax file number declaration

► a superannuation choice form

► a form to collect bank account details for payment of wages

► a confidentiality agreement

► a driver declaration (if driving is required)

► a photo permission slip (if photos are taken for marketing purposes).

You could also include general information for the employee:

► a formal job offer, including details of remuneration and when wages will be paid

▶ information about the business including your business vision, goals and contact numbers

▶ a social club form

▶ occupational health and safety policies

▶ answers to frequently asked questions for employees (yes, you probably won't have many yet, but it is good to prepare the template and allow it to evolve).

Activity 6.5

What forms do you need to prepare for your employee starter pack?

Summary of day 6

Engaging staff or contractors, or outsourcing, is an exciting milestone for growing your small business. Ensure you understand the ongoing costs involved and build them into your budget. Take time to define the goals for the work you want done through documented procedures. Call on experts where necessary and have an appreciation for the responsibilities and obligations that come with growing your business. A great team, in whatever format that may be, can contribute to a great business.

This chapter provided a high-level summary of employer obligations. Remember that your individual circumstances may vary. You should check with the relevant authorities for any recent developments that may be applicable to your business.

On day 7 we will look at launching your business, finding a location for your business, identifying what fit-out your business will require, planning the work flow of the business and putting together a comprehensive business plan.

Day 7

Launching your business

Key areas we will cover on day 7:

► finding a location for your business

► developing procedures manuals

► fitting out your business

► putting together a comprehensive business plan.

I want this chapter to pull everything together for you and give you the confidence and knowledge to launch your own business. Initially we will explore where the business will call home — home office, retail, online or a combination of all three — and what is needed to establish this location. Next, we will examine how to develop procedures manuals, to maintain consistency and quality within the business, and how to potentially utilise them for a franchise venture. Teetering on the edge of launching the business, we will consider where the first client will come from and how to sell to them. Finally and appropriately I will talk about the business plan. I will show you how to put together various elements of the business plan that we have not yet covered in the book so that you have a clear idea of the strategic plans of the business.

Choosing a location

When they think of business, many people conceptualise a traditional high street shop that you visit to purchase products. Is this the sort of business you are thinking of starting? There are many aspects to consider when deciding on a physical location. A suitable location is a critical business decision, and you should look at it from all angles.

What do you need in terms of a business location? Will you expect people to drive to your location to find you, or are you anticipating walking through traffic?

How much space do you require? Is the location easy to find? Is there suitable parking, public transport and disabled accessibility to the area? Do you require loading facilities for stock? Are facilities such as toilets available? You should also look for an area that offers complementary services to your business. If you plan to open a fruit store, you may open next to a butcher or a baker. If you plan to open a store selling cashmere and there is an arcade with four existing shops selling cashmere, that is where you should consider having your location. The arcade is already attracting customers who want to purchase cashmere. If you open in an area where there are no cashmere stores, you may find there is minimal competition, but the local shoppers may also have minimal interest in your store. Remember that finding a cheap lease, a beautiful location or a highly visible location may not mean it is the most profitable location for the store. Consider everything!

When you find what you think is a suitable location, you need to contact the local council to find out about licensing, regulations, zoning and opening hours, details on flood or other acts of Mother Nature that may affect the area, and if there are any developmental changes planned for the area. If there are major roadworks planned right in front of the store, walk-through traffic may be reduced, and this may not suit your business model.

Visit the neighbourhood at different times of day—dawn, mid-morning, mid-afternoon, dinner time and dusk—to assess if there is anything that will affect your decisions. Walk around and talk to local shop owners and people walking by and ask them about the area. Do they think it is a good place for the business you are planning to start? Some leg work in the area can confirm that the location is a great choice, or help you decide not to invest in the area. This may also be your first chance to network and build business relationships with the neighbourhood.

Incorporate the typical council rates, water bills, electricity bills and lease charges into your budget. It seems obvious, but I am mentioning it because many businesses tend to overlook these costs. You need to earn enough income to pay the rent before you even come close to making a profit.

A physical location is also likely to require some sort of fit-out. Fit-outs always seem to cost the business owner far more than initially anticipated. Will you bring an interior designer in or will you plan the fit-out yourself? Can you plan to do the store fit-out in stages; that is, start with the bare minimum, then add some niceties, and finish off with a dream fit-out. It will depend on your business and the clientele you are trying to attract. It is heartbreaking to see people drop hundreds of thousands of dollars on a fit-out only to see the business close down six months later. Consider planning a progressive fit-out so that managing cash flow is easier.

> **Activity 7.1**
>
> What do you need in terms of a business location?

Leasing space

There is nothing like a bricks and mortar shop to declare to the world that you are in business, and a critical step of this process is entering into a lease agreement with the landlord.

If you plan to lease commercial space for your premises, you need to be very clear in your understanding of what the lease terms are, how long the lease will be for and how much money you are committing to. Will annual market or consumer price index (CPI) increases be built into the lease agreement? Do you have the right to renew the lease? What expenses and facilities is the landlord responsible for? Can the leasing agreement be terminated by the landlord, and what notice will they give you? I have worked with retail shops that have spent more than $100 000 on a shop fit-out, only to find the landlord terminated their lease after a year. This makes it very difficult to justify the return on expenditure of the original fit-out expenses.

The rent will increase at a set market rate—for example, 4 per cent—or it will increase based on the consumer price index. Details of the historical consumer price index can be found on the Australian Bureau of Statistics website at www.abr.gov.au.

As an incentive you may be offered, or you may negotiate, an initial period of free rent. Be very careful to plan your cash flow forecasts and put aside money to pay for the full rent once it becomes due. The initial rent-free period is a buffer to help you set up the shop and time to attract clients to your new premises.

Once you start paying rent, it is likely to be nine months before the rent increases in accordance with the lease—another cash-flow consideration.

Before starting the lease you may be required to pay a deposit. The deposit is a non-deductible payment to the landlord, who holds it until the end of the lease when they return the money to the lessee. If there are additional expenses, such as work that needs to be done to return the property to a fit condition for future leasing purposes, the landlord may take that off the deposit, at which time it becomes deductible. At the end of the lease the tenant cannot choose not to pay the final months of rent, because the landlord already has 'their' money.

The lease may include competitive restrictions that stop you selling items that neighbouring shops are selling. For instance, a bakery may not be able to sell drinks if there is a convenience store within the precinct. Likewise, you may want to know and understand what competitive restrictions will be placed on other tenants. If, for example, you are a newsagency selling lottery tickets, you may feel that your sales are affected by charities selling raffle tickets in the courtyard outside your shop.

The lease may include restrictions on when your store may open, or it may require your store to be open at certain times. Landlords usually choose property with a constant flow of foot traffic. Do the stipulated hours suit your business?

The lease may allow you to sublease to other tenants. Subleasing to a complementary business will assist you in paying the rent and increase foot traffic to the store.

A lease is a legal contract between your business and the landlord and you should seek legal advice before signing it to clearly understand what you are financially bound to.

Activity 7.2

- What are the initial and ongoing expenses related to the business location online or offline?

- What licensing and regulation issues do you need to deal with?

- Describe where your business will be located.

- Describe the buy/lease arrangement you have on the location.

The home office

Finding a rent-free space in your house is a cost-effective way to start a business. Many new businesses start their life in the home, on the kitchen table, in a home office or even in a garage. In my local area I have visited dedicated hairdressing studios, nail salons, martial arts studios, boutique dancewear shops, photographic studios and administrative offices set up at home. It's amazing how many thriving home businesses there are in the suburbs that we are unaware of. Will it be suitable to meet clients at your home office, or do you need to establish an alternate venue, like their office, a wi-fi enabled café or serviced offices that hire out by the hour?

You need to check that your home insurance covers you working from home, and covers clients visiting your home office. Depending on the sort of business you are considering operating from home you may need to contact your local council regarding permits or licences. The council is likely to assess how your business will impact on your neighbours in terms of noise disruption and car parking.

Activity 7.3

If you are considering a home office:

- Will your customers visit your premises?

- Will you require a dedicated phone line?

- Do you have suitable insurance in place?

- Are the business's assets secure?

E-commerce

On day 4 we discussed the development of a business's promotional website. Taking this one step further you may be contemplating earning revenue from your website. This is known as **e-commerce**. There are numerous shapes and forms that this can take, from earning 100 per cent of your revenue online or tapping in on an additional online income stream. An online shop for your business could be as simple as setting up a shopfront on eBay (www.ebay.com.au), to a niche site such as Etsy (www.etsy.com.au) for selling handmade goods and crafts, or installing a shopping basket on your website and processing online sales. Other online earning opportunities include selling products, providing online training, advertising, affiliate links and e-books.

The benefits of earning 100 per cent of your income online through a website is that you are location independent: you require neither a home office nor a retail space — just a computer and an internet connection!

The lady who manages a local baby clothes store is always busy, even when the shop is empty. She simultaneously sells the clothing online, and estimates that she generates half her turnover from online sales. You do not have to be a technically savvy geek to venture into online selling! Is an online e-commerce platform something you need to contemplate for your business?

Activity 7.4

Will you contemplate earning income online for your business?

Incubator opportunities

An incubator is a nourishing environment for start-up businesses, generally in the **digital space**. A typical incubator may provide a basic office space that includes a desk, chair, electricity, internet, shared printing and shared facilities. You may be able to rent the space 24/7 or on an hourly basis (or anywhere in between) and you will have access to mentors and advisers, business development support, and have the opportunity to work in a communal area alongside likeminded business owners working through the early stages of the business life cycle. How good does that sound! Australia has a number of incubators that you may be able to access if they suit your business model.

▶ Innovation Centre Sunshine Coast: www.innovation-centre.com.au

▶ River City Labs: www.rivercitylabs.net

▶ Fishburners: www.fishburners.org

▶ Founder Institute: www.fi.co/apply/sydney?secret=preview

▶ PushStart: www.pushstart.com.au

▶ StartPad: www.iaccelerate.com.au/startpad.html

▶ Startup Weekend: www.startupweekend.org

▶ York Butter Factory: www.yorkbutterfactory.com

Even if you don't want to set up home within an incubator, typically they offer opportunities to the public, so keep them on your radar.

Business equipment

When fitting out the office or retail space for your business, think about what you are trying to achieve. It is not a fashion statement: it needs to be a productive, ventilated, safe environment with good lighting and it may need telephone and internet connections and lots of electricity sockets! Fitting out the space does not need to be expensive. Look around at what you already have, and look at second-hand furniture stores and office furniture auctions. There always seems to be a fancy office in town that is refitting where you can pick up offcasts very cheaply.

Your office requires storage space, desks, computers, shredders and other equipment. Plan what you need. Decide if you really need it and where it will go to ensure you don't get too much equipment! Some equipment is redundant these days. I don't have a fax machine because I can send and receive faxes electronically. I use an Australian service called utbox (www .utbox.net). Some equipment now multitasks; for example, most printers now offer photocopying and scanning options. Everything you spend in equipment will come off the profit the business will make, so start frugally and aspire to grow and upgrade.

Activity 7.5

What equipment does your business require?

The paperless office

For many reasons—the environment, back-up security, lack of storage space, improving productivity and minimising retrieval time—I decided to aim for a paperless office. In case you are concerned about maintaining your financial records in a paperless office, ATO Ruling TR 2005/9 stipulates that your electronic financial records may be a true and clear reproduction of the original paper records, as long as they are stored for five years and retrievable at all times. Online accounting software such as XERO enables you to import the source documents as PDFs and store them alongside the journal entry that records the movement of money, for easy retrieval. That sounds pretty cool, doesn't it? No shoeboxes full of receipts for you!

Here are some more tips for developing a paperless office.

▶ Purchase a scanner with optical character recognition (OCR). This enables you to produce a searchable PDF, which allows you to search within the text of what you scan.

▶ Send electronic invoices and encourage your suppliers to send you electronic invoices.

▶ Download CutePDF freeware (www.cutepdf.com), which will enable you to print to PDF and store the document electronically.

▶ For about $15 annually you can buy a digital signature, which will ensure your emails are secure and encrypted.

▶ Sign up to an electronic fax service such as utbox, which enables you to receive and send faxes via email.

Remember, it is vitally important that you store documents securely and in a searchable and retrievable format. To search the documents on my desktop, I use Google Desktop, a free, downloadable piece of software that can search your desktop. I can then click on Google Desktop, type 'insurance' in the search field, and moments later see relevant results from documents, email, Word, Excel or a searchable PDF.

I cannot stress enough the importance of good back-up procedures for your paperless office. Sitting with clients who have paid to have expensive back-up systems installed, and going through the process of retrieving the data only to find it is unreadable—or simply not there—is never enjoyable. On day 2 I mentioned that I use Carbonite and online storage solutions such as Dropbox and Evernote.

Operational strategies

Once you understand what your business will offer, you need to establish how you will produce and deliver your product or service. Will you be dependent on suppliers to deliver the product or raw material? You will need to establish relationships with suppliers, and understand their credit terms and the supply chain. What will they supply? If a manufacturing process is involved, where will the products be manufactured, and will you require plant and equipment for the process? If you are sourcing products from overseas you will have the complexity of dealing with foreign currency.

Activity 7.6

- What suppliers will you be dependent on?

- If the business will undertake a manufacturing process, create a flow chart of the manufacturing process and the activities that will be involved.

Business procedures

If you don't want to **micromanage** and do all the work in your business yourself you need to have systems in place. You will need to build systems around your business's procedures. Employing people is hard, but you will need to get over yourself and your desire to micro control everything. Of course, if issues arise you may have to step in and deal with them, but it is far better to have trained staff, policies and procedures in place detailing step by step how to handle the various situations. This can be formalised in a policy and procedures handbook, which is like a recipe book for your business.

When I lived in Singapore, I worked for a construction company and we went through the process of implementing a quality management system. The system mapped to ISO 9000 business standards as published by the International Organisation for Standardization. Once your business is a reasonable size, this is a journey that you may wish to achieve for your own business. However, during the start-up phase, let's try to keep the development of the business policies and procedures as simple as possible. As mentioned before, developing procedures is like developing a recipe: identify the ingredients, or tools, required and then outline the steps involved in the order they need to be undertaken.

When you start developing your business procedures you may find it useful to develop them within the format of a **wiki**. A wiki enables a team to coordinate and create a collaborative document and it can include images and videos. It can be easily edited by all team members, so everyone can have their own input. When edited, a wiki is like a Word document. When saved, a wiki is like a web page. You can drill down to identify who edited what, when. A well-known wiki is Wikipedia—www .wikipedia.org—a free online encyclopedia to which anyone in the world can contribute. Twiki—www.twiki.org—is an example of a free open source wiki that you can use in your business to help develop business procedures. Giving everyone the opportunity to contribute to the development of business procedures will result in a comprehensive understanding of the processes that are actually taking place in the business.

Activity 7.7

- Do written processes suit your business?
- Which activities could you write business procedures for?

Style guides

The prospect of writing a business procedures handbook can be a bit daunting. The trick is to start by creating a simple style guide. Once you have a style guide, you are in a position to begin recording your business processes, which will in turn develop into a procedures handbook.

A style guide is an overview of how all business communication —including emails, logos, business cards, promotional materials and business procedures manuals—should be produced. It answers all of the questions about how they should look and feel. Pre-formatted templates, ready for editing, could accompany a style guide.

A style guide allows for the generation of simple, consistently branded communication material. Once refined and developed, it can be used for internally or externally prepared material. When you outsource work, you can then provide the job specifications and your business style guide. This saves time and maintains consistency.

Anyone involved in preparing communication material for the business—for example, process writers; virtual assistants; and advertising, marketing and graphic design consultants—can refer to the style guide, and it can be used internally or externally.

A style guide typically answers the following questions.

▶ What is the font style and size for the different styles that may be needed—for example, Normal, Heading 1, Heading 2?

▶ What is the standard format for a footer and header?

▶ What are the company colours?

▶ What are the margin specifications?

▶ What border size should be selected for images?

▶ What alignment should be used?

▶ What spacing should there be between paragraphs?

▶ When should bullet points be used?

▶ What language should be used?

▶ How should the business name be written?

▶ What are the permitted ways to use the trademark?

Figure 7.1 is an example of different responses to the question, 'What language should be used?'

Figure 7.1: a style guide should answer questions such as, 'What language should be used?'

Simple response	Use plain Australian English.
Detailed response	Select English (Australia), use plain English and choose simple terms over complex phrases. Use more verbs and fewer nouns. Use short sentences. Use the same words and patterns. Don't use synonyms. The response could go on to provide acceptable nouns, verbs and abbreviations; standard, commonly used terminology; and preferred key words for search engine optimisation.

Your style guide needs to allow for the development of easy-to-follow business procedures. Start simply and develop it further as you need it. Once it's created, you're ready to start tinkering with the first edition of your business procedures handbook.

Activity 7.8

Answering the following questions will help you start creating a style guide for your business.

- What is the font style and size for Normal, Heading 1 and Heading 2 (and so on)?

- What is the standard format for a footer and header?

- What are the company colours?

- What are the margin specifications?

- What border size should be selected for images?

- What alignment should be used?

- What spacing should there be between paragraphs?

- When should bullet points be used?

- What language should be used?

Formalising procedures

The development of a business procedures handbook is like the chicken and the egg. Which comes first: the work or the procedures handbook? In reality you start on the first draft and tinker with the procedures, adapting them to business and client requirements, new laws and technology developments. They are a living and evolving business document.

To explain what I mean by business procedures, if, for instance, you were a medical practitioner, your procedure for visiting a patient might be:

▶ Within the first minute the patient sits down...

▶ During the second minute you open their electronic file...

▶ By the fifth minute you have enquired about their health...

and so on. The procedures you create have to guide your employees through what you expect them to do, and the time frame in which you expect it done.

This particular business procedure may seem unlikely; however, it is taken from a real-life example of a professional in a now large and successful practice. She implemented the procedure when she wanted to grow her practice. This is a great example of standardising a service, although I realise that it is not for everyone. My own doctor quit his practice when they tried to introduce this sort of micromanagement. He could never keep within the time limits, his consults always ran late and there were long waiting periods to see him.

If you want to grow a business, you need to manage your costs and you need to be aware of any staff who take longer than others to carry out a procedure. Why is this? Do they need training? Do they suit the business that you are trying to grow? If some staff are going to run long appointments, should the business charge extra for their services, to cover the extra expense of their time?

I worked with one small business that had a considerably high staff turnover. This is a clear sign that something is wrong with the existing business model. A high staff turnover reflects poor morale and is expensive for the business, as it has to continually invest money in recruiting and retraining new staff.

I explored the possible reasons behind the high staff turnover of the small, busy café. Their time-poor owner said some staff just knew what to do, and how to plate up a meal, and some staff didn't. They were adding an extra serve of fish at five dollars apiece or an extra serve of chips to a plate, which was eating into profits. If kitchen staff did not plate up properly, then the café was effectively paying the patrons to eat there!

Rather than invest in training, the business decided that the staff who did not know how to plate up a meal correctly would not be rostered on again. As a result, new staff members were frequently brought in. The result was confusion about procedures, minimal time spent on training and a stressed boss, all which was contributing to low morale in the workplace — not a good business model, and very emotionally stressful for everyone.

Written procedures within small businesses are very useful; however, a picture says 1000 words. The solution was that the kitchen staff needed to know exactly what each meal should look like. So the owner took photos of each dish as it should appear, and pinned the photos up in the kitchen. Underneath each photo he listed exactly what should be on the plate. The business defined what the staff should prepare in the photos and the staff knew what to serve. Café staff were able to compare the visual images, and read what should be on each plate with what they were serving during the bustling café operations.

I have also heard of business owners videoing procedures. Business owners can video procedures and upload them to a secure website for viewing by the employee, or email them to virtual assistants.

Utilising a business policies and procedures handbook will ensure the steps carried out for a process are the same each time, which should result in consistent outcomes.

Use the business procedures handbook to coordinate in-house checklists, templates, processes, images and videos. Once the business is in operation the developed business procedures will in turn assist in streamlining the processes.

Activity 7.9

- What processes in your business can you photograph?
- What processes in your business can you video?

Franchising your business

A franchise is a structure where a franchisor's successful and branded business model is replicated and licensed to a franchisee. There are various legal structures for the franchise relationship. It is a means of rapidly growing your business as the franchisee invests their own money and they in turn have a vested interest in the running of the business. As the franchisor you would provide training, support, promotional activity and detailed guidance on how to run the operations to the franchisees. Detailed guidance could come in the form of a procedures handbook. Although you are in the early days of starting your small business, it is strategic to understand the goals you have for your business and to develop your business with those goals in mind.

Before you give up your day job

You need to consider the revenue the business will generate and the cash reserves that you have in place to finance the venture. Initially you may have to work on the business after hours. Once it is generating an income flow, you could reduce your paid working hours; and then leave your job altogether when your business is generating enough income to cover your income needs or — better still — when it becomes self-sufficient and runs itself. You should clearly understand what your own personal expenses are and what sort of income you need to generate to replace your salary or wage. If you are a mumpreneur or a greypreneur you may not have the same considerations.

> **Activity 7.10**
>
> What do you need to consider before taking a leap of faith and quitting your job?

Juggling the business and your life

Many a business has started up after a parent found that the rigid 9-to-5 work life did not suit their life with children. I've found a symbiotic relationship can develop between a parent and a child within the framework of such a business.

If you involve your kids in your work they provide rich and varied opportunities for you to meet fellow parents and carers; for example, basketball, netball, dancing classes, playgroups and art classes. You never know who you might meet at the sand box: your next sales opportunity, a technical resource, an SEO expert — even a potential investor.

Children can be taught some of the simple administrative tasks such as label making, designing Christmas cards, simple data entry, putting stamps on envelopes, putting files in alphabetical order, and answering the phone and taking messages.

Promote that you are family friendly. Prospective clients have called and asked if it would be okay if they breastfeed in front of me. Of course, that's not for everyone, but I see it as an advantage — something working in my favour. I am family friendly and I don't necessarily want to work for clientele who don't share those values.

Allowing your child to be exposed to your small business is immensely beneficial for them: it is educational, it may provide them with some pocket money and it enables them to see you—the parent—in a different light. As parents we are tired, we are juggling and we lack the valuable commodity of time. It is encouraging to realise that in many ways our children can be a positive resource for our business if we let them.

Finding your first client or customer

Triumphant validation of your business may come when you make your first sale to a client or customer. Prior to finding their first customer or client I have known several of my clients offer family and friends free products in return for feedback on the sales process so they could sort out any unexpected issues. Once you are ready to sell your product or service, it may be daunting to contemplate where you will find your first paying client. Don't be too proud. Launching a business is hard work. You may think everything is in place and then find you need to start door knocking, ringing past colleagues or arranging coffees with friends to make your first sale. Every business had to start somewhere. These are the stories you can share when your business is a roaring success. Making your first sale will enable you to monitor if you have a streamlined supply and delivery process firmly in place before the general public starts knocking at your door.

The business plan

The purpose of a business plan is to provide focus and direction for business owners and shareholders. A business plan should communicate to the stakeholders what they need to know about the business and why they should invest in the business. It provides an overview of what the business is about, who the business will sell to, where the business will sell and the make-up of the business team.

A conventional business book would have started with 'Day 1: Develop a Business Plan'. But, fortunately for both of us, this is not a conventional business book! Working at the coal face with small business owners, I realise that the task of writing a business plan is daunting, overwhelming and easy to cast aside.

So, I have broken down and explained many of the elements of a business plan and weaved them through this book. If you go to appendix A (on p. 193), you will see a structured business plan template. The activities you completed as you read through the book simply slot into the business plan template. Before you know it, you will have a rich, informative and strategic foundation for a successful business.

Your business plan should expand on how your business intends to grow over the next five years or even longer. I have read that Chinese business plans can be 300 years long, and include detailed succession plans when the business plan is handed down through the generations.

A business plan may be written on the back of a drinks coaster or it may be a comprehensive document. I think it is useful to spend some time working through and considering the different elements of your business before diving in with a bag of money, eyes wide shut. Include graphics or images in your business plan if that helps you explain aspects.

Over the next few pages I am going to discuss the various elements of a business plan that have not yet been covered. As I mentioned, while working through the book, you have had the opportunity of completing activities, and your answers to the questions can be slotted very easily into your own business plan. How do you eat an elephant? One bite at a time. My thinking is that by breaking down the elements of the business plan along the way you would feel more confident to pull your own plan together using the relevant content we have covered over the past seven days.

Vision statement

Business books love to tell you that you need a vision statement and a mission statement for your business plan. In reality it seems many businesses have either not invested the time in developing these statements, or they have kind of merged them into one. My advice to you is to think about them, but don't get bogged down in the detail.

A vision statement is a motivational and inspiring picture of the business's future, but it does not describe how you are going to get there. It provides a focused framework for strategic and business planning and it will challenge the business to achieve specific outcomes.

Activity 7.11

What will the vision statement for your business be?

Mission statement

A mission statement describes how the business's vision will be achieved. It may be loosely considered that the vision statement is for internal use while the mission statement is for external interested parties.

Visit Australia Post to see a clear example of vision and mission statements: www.auspost.com.au/about-us/vision-mission.html.

Goals and objectives

On day 1 we talked about business goals, to start you thinking about why you are starting a business. Goals and objectives need to align with the business vision and mission to motivate staff to achieve them. A goal is a statement of what the business hopes to achieve, while objectives are what you need to do to help you achieve your goals. Goals can be centred on profitability, sales targets, process improvement, customer satisfaction, market share—anything that will move the business towards its vision. The objectives are the steps you need to take towards achieving the business goals. Now, on day 7, you should have a clearer idea of what the business vision is and how you can establish goals that correspond with that vision.

Action plan

The action plan is a detailed outline of the tasks that need to be undertaken to achieve the objectives and in turn the mission and the vision of the business. To help you crystallise and work through your action plan, you can use the online project management tool Trello (www.trello.com) or download the hierarchical ToDoList from www.abstractspoon.com.

Trello allows you to break a project down into any number of defined 'To Do' lists of activities. As you work on the activities, you move the activity into the 'Doing' list, and once the activity is completed you move the activity into the 'Done' list. As it is an online tool you can invite other users to collaborate on Trello and assign task activities to the other users.

ToDoList is a PC-based project management tool that enables you to repeatedly subdivide activities. As with Trello, all of the activities can be allocated to other members of the team, and the activities can also be allocated colour and time references to assist in highlighting their priority.

With a bit of intuition you should have both of them up and running in no time.

Activity 7.14

What is the action plan for your business?

SWOT analysis

A SWOT analysis is a grid analysis comparing the strengths, weaknesses, opportunities and threats for the business. Understanding this diagnosis will enable you to leverage off your strengths and opportunities and tackle your weaknesses and threats. In addition, a SWOT analysis can assist you in developing an action plan for the business. For example, if a lack of sales experience within the proposed team is a perceived weakness, you can look at hiring a sales professional or having your staff undergo sales training to deal with the issue.

Activity 7.15

Complete a SWOT analysis for your business.

Strengths	Weaknesses
Opportunities	Threats

Key performance indicators (KPIs)

Key performance indicators or (KPIs) are a means of measuring and monitoring the performance of a business. To effectively use KPIs you need to carefully select KPIs that tie in with the strategic goals of your business. Then you need to select individual targets for the KPIs, and clearly understand what results you want to achieve in order to keep aligned with reaching the business's strategic goals. Monitoring the healthy results of KPIs should be an indication the business is on track, while unhealthy results highlight areas in the business that may need further attention. Identifying shortfalls gives you opportunities to target areas of the business that need your attention.

Financial KPIs include such areas as activity, asset usage, cash flow, coverage, efficiency, gearing, growth, liquidity and profitability.

Non-financial KPIs can be developed to suit the needs of the business and may include business development, customer service, marketing, operations, personnel and sales.

There is a plethora of ratios available to measure and monitor the business against.

Financial KPIs

Here are a few financial KPIs you may wish to consider for your business.

Profitability KPIs

Profitability KPIs include:

► *Total sales turnover.* The total income earned by the company compared across periods. By comparing the total income earned across similar periods, you can see a trend in the actual dollars received by the business.

► *Gross profit margin (%) or gross margin.* The proportion of income that is left after deducting all of the costs related to the cost of goods sold. This indicates whether you will cover expenses and in turn make a profit from the average mark-up you are applying to products or services. It is useful to apply it to the company overall, and to look at individual product margins. If the gross profit margin is 50 per cent for every dollar the company earns selling its products or services, it has 50 cents left over.

Activity KPIs

Activity KPIs include:

► *Average debtors days.* The average number of days it will take the business to collect outstanding payments from clients or customers. A low number is favourable; a high number indicates inefficiency in collecting debts or potential bad debts.

▶ *Average creditor days.* The average number of days it will take the business to pay outstanding payments to suppliers. A high number is favourable; however, you need to pay your bills by the due date otherwise you may find suppliers will no longer service you.

Liquidity KPIs

Liquidity KPIs include current ratio (or liquidity ratio); that is, comparing the total current assets with the current liabilities. This is a measure of the business's ability to pay its debts over the next 12 months. If the ratio is below 1, then the company may have difficulty meeting short-term obligations.

Gearing: debt-to-equity ratio KPIs

The debt-to-equity ratio is a measure of the total liabilities, borrowings or debt in proportion to the owner's investment in the company. A high ratio means that the borrowings of the business are high, and future borrowings may be restricted, which means the ratio remains high.

Efficiency KPIs

Efficiency includes billing hours per week versus total hours available to work in the period—the higher the number, the greater the hours that have been billed during the period.

Cash-flow KPIs

This is the operating cash-flow ratio; that is, the cash generated by the operating activities of the business. This ratio is a measure of how liquid the firm is in the short term and the business's abilities to pay its debts.

Growth KPIs

Growth includes leads generated versus leads converted. This is an indication of how effective the sales team is at converting leads to sales.

Break-even analysis KPIs

This is the sales required to cover expenses—in simplistic terms, what the sales need to be to have a profit of zero. You can look at this on a whole company basis, or at an individual product level. I used to buy coffee from a vendor who knew that by the time he had sold 250 coffees in the day, he had reached a breakeven point, and after that he was earning a profit. He monitored this daily, and it motivated him to achieve sales targets. It was a lot easier to pour the 251st cup of coffee because he knew he was making money from that one.

Non-financial KPIs

There are also a few non-financial KPIs you may like to consider for your business.

Customer-service KPIs

It's good to haves a system to monitor the number of complaints a business receives. It enables the business to implement improvements to ensure no further complaints are received. Ideally you do not want to receive any complaints; however, you also need to ensure the business has a channel for receiving feedback.

Occupational health and safety KPIs

Occupational health and safety KPIs include monitoring the number of accidents occurring on the worksite. The ideal number is zero and anything more than this should be investigated, and improvements implemented if necessary.

Human resources KPIs

You can monitor the total number of hours staff take as paid days absent as a total, or compare this to the total number of hours worked to calculate the absenteeism rate. Staff absenteeism reduces productivity and a high ratio may be an indication of poor staff morale or an unhealthy work environment.

Sales KPIs

Sales KPIs give you an indication of the average value of a sale a typical customer makes for the business. Some customers will buy a significant amount from your business while other customers will only buy a small amount. You want to identify the customers who spend above average sales with you, and ensure the relationships are nourished. You also want to check that potential above average spending customers are identified and marketed to. This will ensure the return on investment of your marketing dollar is utilised in the most effective manner.

Marketing KPIs

These are the number of qualified leads—the total numbers of potential customers suited to your business that meet buying criteria and have expressed an interest in the products or services on offer, which makes them likely to become your customers.

Operations KPIs

Operations KPIs monitor on-time delivery. As the name suggests, this ratio gives an indication of the delivery performance of goods or services the business provides. If it is good, this ratio is used in promotions to demonstrate that outcomes will be delivered on the quoted due date as customers may be logistically dependent on the delivery time. Customers may prefer to purchase from a business with a consistent on-time delivery outcome.

Even though I have listed only a few KPIs here you can see that they cover a wide spectrum of the business operations. You can select well-known ratios or customise ratios to suit the needs of your business. To effectively use KPIs they should be featured on your 'business dashboard'. A business dashboard may take many forms: it may be an Excel spreadsheet or it may be a part of your accounting software. Like a car dashboard, you should be able to glance at the business dashboard to monitor that you are on track to meet strategic goals.

The accounting software XERO has a six-page Management Report feature, while MYOB has an interactive Business Insights feature. These both work like a business dashboard; however, if you want a powerful, easy-to-use business dashboard look at the online software tool called Fathom (www.FathomHQ.com), which offers practically everything you could want from a business dashboard: numerical, graphical, interactive management reporting and financial analysis, which includes both financial and non-financial KPIs. It will also integrate with your data from Excel, XERO and MYOB. If you want to grow a large business or franchise empire, this is definitely a tool that you need to explore.

You can visit my website for details of more KPIs you could apply to your business.

Activity 7.16

Which key performance indicators can be used to assist you in achieving the goals of your business?

External environment

There are external factors over which your business may have no control, but that will nevertheless have a direct impact on the business. Legislation relating to tax or the industry the business operates in may affect business decisions. There are also external economic business indicators that the business may have to consider.

The business plan should identify external factors such as interest rates, consumer price index (CPI) and retail sales that are relevant to the business and incorporate them into the planning. The Australian Bureau of Statistics has the economic indicators available on their website at www.abs.gov.au.

Activity 7.17

Which external factors does your business need to be aware of and why?

Company story

What is the story behind the business? In order for people to connect, you should be able to eloquently share your business story. What was the inspirational spark behind starting your business? Maybe it started when you picked up this book, or when you were made redundant from that job you hated. Or perhaps it started when you were eight years old and obsessed with making a mess in the kitchen in the name of creating cup cakes.

Sharing the story behind creating the endeavour will assist in providing focus and answering other questions about what the business aims to achieve. As well as ending up in the business plan, the company story is compelling marketing material.

> ### Activity 7.18
> What is your company story?

Key activities

It makes sense that the business plan should outline the key activities of the business that are necessary to implement the business plan. What will the business initially focus its activities on? What will the business sell? Will the business develop its own private label or sell brands? What are the optimal service products the business will offer? The desirable outcomes of the key activities should be monitored to ensure the business remains focused on achieving strategic goals.

> ### Activity 7.19
> What are the key activities of the business?

Management team

In your business plan, include a brief description of the management team that will be involved with the business. Detail their experience, specialties, qualifications and the skills they bring to the business. This will aid you in understanding what additional skills and expertise are required in the business. These skills and expertise will need to be hired or outsourced, and the additional expense needs to be built into the business budget.

Activity 7.20

Outline the business management team and detail their experience, specialties, qualifications and skills relevant to the business.

Worst-case scenario

You need to hope for the best and plan for the worst. If the business is not a success, what will you lose? If you divert your mortgage into the business, could you lose your family home? Likewise, if you invest your parents' mortgage and retirement funds into the business, they may end up living with you! If your office is broken into, you have a fire or flood, or a hacker attacks your website, do you have offsite back-ups in place? Are you prepared for the worst-case scenario? Develop a disaster recovery plan and prudently consider these questions. A disaster recovery plan is an outline of policies and procedures the business will undertake to recover or continue operations in a seamless manner when faced with disaster. The plan will include details about back-ups and IT recovery, insurance and a financing buffer. A business that does not know how to overcome obstacles will go out of business. Spend the time to consider this so you are fully prepared.

Activity 7.21

Outline what should be included in your business recovery plan for your own business.

Summary of day 7

Congratulations! You have reached the end of the book and the start of a new chapter in your life and your business. I am so excited for you. If you have worked your way through this book you should be in an enlightened position to know what you need to do.

It is delusional to think that if you dedicate long hours to doing what you are passionate about you will succeed, as you need to be clear and focused on how your business will make money. Pull your plan together, work through any critical gaps, talk to people, network and smash any feelings of analysis paralysis. Don't let small set-backs get you down: failure is the stepping stone to success. Stay positive! Pull together the tasks you need to achieve the goals of starting your business.

Creating a business does not necessarily mean that you have to work outside your comfort zone. It is easy to be motivated by guerrilla marketing techniques of business coaches encouraging you to reach for the stars, and spend and expand. But big is not always better. I liken small businesses to a windsurfer, and big business to a cruise ship. As a small business we can make decisions quickly and work towards our goals; however, if an unexpected opportunity arises we can quickly adjust our course. A cruise ship, while robust, takes a long time to react to new opportunities.

Focus on establishing a business that can cope with and grow with success. Too much success can crush a business because it may grow beyond its means.

You will need to be prepared for the tough days, long working weeks, dealing with bad debts, disgruntled employees or aggressive competitors. It has been said that an entrepreneur is someone who works a 16-hour day so they can generate passive income when they sleep. Establish mechanisms to keep yourself strong and soldier on through the difficult times. This may involve discussions with your mentor, communicating with your small business banking specialist, taking a short break, journalising or blogging your woes or even Pilates. Whatever it takes, have something in place. I can vouch that chocolate and chardonnay are not always the answer!

Don't allow yourself to become too emotionally attached to the original business model. Share early, share often and prototype fast so you will be able to evolve your business model into something the market wants and will reward you for.

The first business that you start may not be a corporate empire, but you will learn so much from the practical application of starting and running a business. This knowledge, skills and experience will help you start or evolve into a larger business if you want to. One day, running your business will teach you more than many books and courses combined.

Good luck on your journey,

Heather Smith

Appendix A

Business plan template

Use the activities that you have completed as you worked your way through the book to complete the business plan below. Enter as much information as you want.

Business name

Enter the name of your business.

Vision statement

Activity 7.11

What will the vision statement for your business be?

Mission statement

Activity 7.12

What will the mission statement for your business be?

Business goals

Activity 1.1

What are your personal SMART goals for running a business? Remember to address specific, measurable, attainable, realistic and timely goal criteria.

Activity 7.13

What are the goals for your business?

Business objectives

Activity 7.13

What are the objectives for your business?

Company story

Activity 7.18

What is your company story?

Key activities

Activity 7.19

What are the key activities of the business?

Business profile

Activity 2.5

What will your registered business name be?

Activity 2.6

Does your business name have a story behind it?

Activity 2.7

- Is your chosen business name available on the IP Australia website database, ATMOSS?

- Do you have a business name that needs to be trademarked?

Activity 4.8

What is the registered domain name of your business?

Activity 2.2

- What is your registered ABN?

- What is your ACN?

Activity 2.4

On which date will your business commence?

Activity 7.1

What do you need in terms of a business location?

Activity 7.2

Describe where your business will be located.

Describe the buy/lease arrangement you have on the location.

Activity 2.3

What is the chosen legal structure of the business?

Management profile

Activity 2.3

Who will have ownership of the business?

Activity 6.1

Outline the anticipated organisation chart for your business.

Activity 7.20

Outline the business management team and detail their experience, specialties, qualifications and skills relevant to the business.

Activity 3.3

- Would you benefit from the expertise of a business coach?

- Would you benefit from the expertise of a business mentor?

- Will your business have an advisory board? Who will be on it?

Activity 1.2

- What personality traits do you have that are suited to starting a business?

- Are there gaps in your knowledge? Would you benefit from additional training?

- What relevant experience do you bring to the business?

Action plan

Activity 7.14

What is the action plan for your business?

Activity 4.1

Will your business be affected by seasonal fluctuations?

Products or services the business offers

Activity 1.4

What products or services will your business sell?

Activity 7.6

- What suppliers will you be dependent on?

- If the business will undertake a manufacturing process, create a flow chart of activities relevant to the business.

Activity 7.15

Complete a SWOT analysis for your business.

Strengths	Weaknesses
Opportunities	Threats

Activity 5.3

- How will you price the products/services you have on offer?

- How will your prices compare with your competition's?

Product or service	Our price	Competitor price (range)

Activity 7.16

Which key performance indicators can be used to assist you in achieving the goals of your business?

Staffing

Activity 6.3

Do you know which pay awards will be appropriate for your staff?

Activity 6.4

Have you selected a default superannuation fund for your business?

Market research

Activity 1.5

- Does your business idea have merit?

- Is there a demand for the products or services you plan to sell?

Activity 1.8

- Do you see any trends within your industry and will your business be able to take advantage of them?

- Describe the current market environment (refer to current population levels, employee availability, the economy and recent trends). Where will your business fit in this environment?

Activity 1.6

- What profile do you have of the business's ideal customer?

- What market research can you do to assess the viability of your business concept?

Activity 1.7

- Do you understand what competitive advantages and disadvantages your business has? Why are you better than your competitors?

Competitor	Overview of competitor	Perceived strengths and weaknesses of competitor?	What are their prices? How do your products compare?	How will your business be better than your competitors'?

- Why will your customers or clients prefer to purchase products or services from your business rather than from your competitors?

Competitor profile

Activity 4.7

- Who are your competitors?

- What size are they?

- Where are they located?

- What services do they offer?

- How will your business be different from its competitors?

Legal, regulation, licence and insurance requirements for the business

Activity 3.1

- What legislation may impact the running of your business?

- What areas of your business will you get a small-business lawyer to assist you with?

Activity 3.4

- Circle the insurances will you need to consider for your business:

  public liability   professional indemnity
  product liability   business assets
  business revenue   workers' compensation
  tax audit.

- Complete this risk-management table (overleaf).

What risks could impact on your business?	How will you minimise possible risk to the business?

Activity 2.1

What licences, permits, registrations and certificates does your business potentially require? (Include a table of what you have and what you will need.)

Activity 3.9

- Will your business negatively impact the environment or local community?

- What environmental measures can your business adopt to ensure environmentally friendly behaviour?

Promotion

Activity 4.2

What colours will you choose for your business?

Colour	CMYK (cyan, magenta, yellow, black)	RGB (red, green, blue)	Hex (hexadecimal)
e.g. Brown	C 0.0000 M 0.0000 Y 0.2000 K 0.6670	858568	#555544

Activity 4.5

- What CRM will you use in your business?

- Why will past customers come back to your business?

- Will you have a customer loyalty or referrals program to encourage repeat business?

Activity 4.3

What ideas do you have for a business logo?

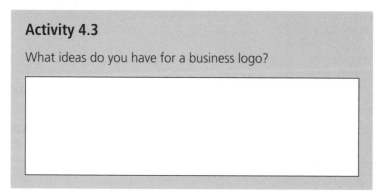

Activity 4.6

- Will you prepare a newsletter for your business?

- How often will you send out newsletters?

Activity 4.9

Which social media profiles will you create for your business?

Activity 4.1

- Will your business be affected by seasonal fluctuations?

- Are there any significant dates in the calendar when your business can anticipate higher than average sales? Will you have the capacity to deliver?

Market risks

Activity 7.17

Which external factors does your business need to be aware of and why?

Activity 7.21

Outline what should be included in your business recovery plan for your own business.

Business equipment

Activity 7.5

What equipment does your business require?

Activity 3.6

- What hardware will you require for your business?
- How will you procure it? (cash, credit or leasing)
- How much will this cost you?

Activity 3.7

- What software do you require for your business?
- How much will it cost you?

Finance

Activity 5.1

- What funds do you need to invest into your business before you can start trading?

- What personal funds do you estimate you will require for the first year of your business?

Activity 5.5

Prepare a 12-month profit and loss budget for the business.

Activity 5.2

- Will you register for the Goods and Services Tax (GST)?

- On what date will your business be registered for the GST?

Activity 3.2

- Will you do the bookkeeping yourself, hire a bookkeeper or outsource bookkeeping?

- Will you do the tax accounting yourself or hire the services of a tax accountant?

- Do you want the tax accountant to assist only with basic taxation compliance or will they be a financial adviser to the business as well?

Activity 7.2

What are the initial and ongoing expenses related to the business location online or offline?

Innovation

Activity 3.5

- Will your business have intellectual property?

- How will you protect your intellectual property?

- Do you intend to have designs, patents or trademarks that you will need to register appropriately?

- Do you need to put non-disclosure agreements in place?

Appendix B

Business plan for Mulrenan Gardeners

Here is an example fictional business plan for Mulrenan Gardeners. You will see that it maps to some of the activities in this book. Some activities, such as those related to marketing, have been merged. Other activities, such as those related to innovation, are not relevant to this business so they have been omitted.

Your business plan is what you make of it — it is what *you* need from a business plan. The purpose of writing a business plan is to help you understand the viability of the business you are starting, consider the business from all angles and clarify the financial requirements of the business.

Business name

Mulrenan Gardeners

Vision statement

Mulrenan Gardeners is committed to providing high-quality household gardening services to the local Bulimba area, in a sustainable and environmentally friendly manner.

Mission statement

We will meet our customers' needs by:

▶ employing friendly, trained and knowledgeable staff

▶ utilising modern, serviced equipment

▶ offering competitive pricing

▶ understanding the local environment and adapting to seasonal fluctuations

▶ monitoring our carbon footprint.

Business goals and objectives

The goals of Mulrenan Gardeners are to:

▶ provide a bi-monthly service to 60 households in the local area, within one year of commencing operations

▶ ensure all staff will be certified to a minimum of Certificate IV in Horticulture within six months of engagement

▶ develop and maintain a profitable business, with a positive cash flow, within three months of commencing operations

▶ develop an appreciation of local flora and be perceived as the experts to turn to for sustainable gardening, within two years of commencing operations.

Company story

Mulrenan Gardeners is a partnership consisting of three brothers who are passionate about environmentally efficient practices. Over a drink at the local sailing club, they decided to start a gardening business that would encourage the community to adopt earth-friendly practices in their own backyard. Each brother brings to the business different skills and experiences, and together they aim to grow a family-friendly work environment.

Key activities

The business's key activities include:

▶ mowing

▶ gardening

▶ fertilising

▶ mulching

▶ weed control.

Business profile

Business name: Mulrenan Gardeners

The company is named after the three founding brothers. Literally translated, the name 'Mulrenan' means descendants of the water god Rian, which is appropriate for a gardening business.

Registered business name: Mulrenan Gardeners Pty Ltd

The business name is available on the IP Australia website database, ATMOSS.

Registered domain name: www.MulrenanGardeners.com.au

The domain name 'Mulrenan' is already used so we have chosen to use 'MulrenanGardeners' and only have the .com.au extension.

Registered Australian Business Number: 12 756 651 23X

Australian Company Number: 756 651 23X

Business commencement date: Mulrenan Gardeners aims to commence business in July 2012.

Business location

Mulrenan Gardeners will run a mobile operation. A truck will be used to store transportable equipment, and will be driven to each serviced location. Bruce Mulrenan will set up a home office as a central place for all administrative tasks. Andrew Mulrenan will house all excess equipment for the gardening operations.

While the business establishes itself, it will not lease any premises.

Legal structure of the business

The founders opted for a proprietary limited legal structure for the business as they wanted to ensure their personal assets were separated and protected from the business. Bruce is a lawyer, so he was able to take care of the legal matters of the business at a reasonable cost.

Management profile

Business owners: The business will be jointly owned by brothers Bruce, Andrew and Cameron Mulrenan.

Bruce Mulrenan (age 27 years) is:

► a practising environmental lawyer

► studying a Certificate IV in Horticulture.

Andrew Mulrenan (age 25 years):

► runs a landscaping business

► holds a diploma in horticulture.

Cameron Mulrenan (age 23 years):

- ► has completed a business degree
- ► is studying a Certificate IV in Horticulture
- ► has accounting experience
- ► has earned money mowing lawns since he was 16 years old.

Organisation chart for the business

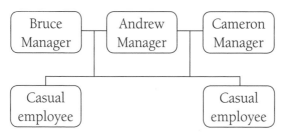

Advisory board

The brothers have consulted with their parents, Jim Jones (a retired landscaper) and their accountant about mentoring their developing business. This advisory board plans to have a strategic meeting at the accountant's office once every six months.

Initially the business will not engage a business coach; however, Cameron has decided to engage a business coach to work with him personally. As he is younger he hopes this will make up for his lack of experience.

The brothers are competitive high achievers who work well together. Growing up they ran a paper delivery business and a car washing business in their local neighbourhood, and have always discussed the possibility of running another business together.

Experience gaps

▶ Cameron and Bruce are studying to complete a Certificate IV in Horticulture.

▶ Bruce is thinking about getting some casual work with a gardening business to enhance his understanding of the gardening business.

▶ There are some courses on caring for organic gardens that they are interested in attending.

▶ Cameron wants further training in using an accounting solution.

▶ They will need to up-skill on the latest fertilising techniques.

Action plan

▶ Cameron and Bruce will complete their Certificate IV in Horticulture within six months.

▶ A suitable truck will be purchased, and a vinyl sticker of the company's logo will be organised.

▶ Branding and logo for the business will be developed.

▶ Bank accounts for the business will be opened.

▶ Before we commence operation, we are considering running a survey on our Facebook page to assist in determining pricing of the services that we will offer.

Marketing calendar

	J	A	S	O	N	D	J	F	M	A	M	J
	Winter		Spring			Summer			Autumn			Winter
Monthly Newsletter	Monthly N'letter	Monthly N'letter	Monthly N'letter	Monthly N'letter	Monthly N'letter	Monthly N'letter	Monthly N'letter	Monthly N'letter	Monthly N'letter	Monthly N'letter	Monthly N'letter	Monthly N'letter
Radio			Radio spot to inform people what they need to do for the start of the season			Radio spot to inform people what they need to do for the start of the season			Radio spot to inform people what they need to do for the start of the season			Radio spot to inform people what they need to do for the start of the season
Ekka promotion		Gardening themed show bag is given away with every booking										
Advertising	Advertise in the local paper			Advertise in the local paper			Advertise in the local paper			Advertise in the local paper		

The advertising will cost $200 per quarter. All other marketing activities will consume time, but are free.

Products and services the business offers

The business will offer the following services:

▶ mowing

▶ gardening

▶ fertilising

▶ mulching

▶ weed control.

Andrew Mulrenan runs a landscaping business. A commission will be earned by Mulrenan Gardeners for any new client of Mulrenan Gardeners who uses Andrew's landscaping business.

SWOT analysis

Strengths	Weaknesses
• All directors are physically strong and healthy. • They know the local area and many members of the community.	• The brothers will continue to work in their corporate roles so they can only focus on the company part of the time. This means it may be slow growing the business. • The business has no existing client base.
Opportunities	**Threats**
• The brothers grew up in the neighbourhood and are well known in the local community. • There is a trend towards sustainability.	• Wet weather reduces the time when services can be offered. • Rezoning of the area to high density would mean a reduction in the number of gardens in the area.

Pricing

Pricing is a challenge because competitors do not promote their prices. We are thinking of initially pricing according to the service, be it mowing, mulching, fertilising, and so on. In the local areas, it seems that there is an hourly rate ranging from $30 to $85.

Mulrenan Gardeners believes that if it has the skills and the correct equipment available, it can do the work more quickly than its competitors can, and thus it does not want to offer a low hourly rate. There also seems to be a tendency in the industry to quote via job, rather than hourly. We are looking at ways to assist us in determining a methodology for job quoting, and feel that this will come with time and experience. The area sizes of the local gardens are 16 perch (405 square metres), 24 perch (607 square metres) and 32 perch (809 square metres) and we will collect this information for each job. The area size should correlate with the amount of work required at the property.

Key performance indicators

▶ *Income earned per garden*. To maximise profitability Mulrenan Gardeners will monitor the income they generate from each address and focus on upselling to their client base.

▶ *Gross profit growth*. To maximise profitability the gross profit growth every month will be monitored. Formula: (current gross profit less previous period gross profit) divided by previous period gross profit.

▶ *Accounts receivable days*. To assist in monitoring cash flow, and to ensure the business is paid promptly, the accounts receivable days will be monitored and compared with the company credit terms. Formula: average gross receivables divided by (net sales divided by 365).

Staffing

Under Modern Awards, Fair Work Australia's 'Horticulture Award 2010' may apply to staff.

Default superannuation fund for the business

Sunsuper

Market research

A survey of local residents was conducted at the local shops in Bulimba. Respondents were asked if they used or would use a gardening service. Sixty-two per cent of respondents said they had a garden and 30 per cent said they would consider having a regular gardening service, while 25 per cent said they would hire a gardener on a part-time basis.

A targeted advertisement was run on Facebook channelling people to the Mulrenan Gardeners Facebook page where again they were asked to complete a survey, which was created using Survey Monkey. Fifty-eight per cent of respondents said they had a garden and 37 per cent said they would consider having a regular gardening service, while 30 per cent said they would hire a gardener on a part-time basis. The additional benefit of running this survey is that we now have an interested community on our Facebook page.

We realise that survey respondents do not always translate into real practice; however, we feel that this indicates a healthy interest in the services we are offering.

Bulimba area

Source: Map data © 2012 GBRMPA, Google, Whereis®, Sensis Pty Ltd.

Ideal customer

Our ideal customer:

▶ has a garden in Bulimba or the surrounding areas

▶ has a garden with at least 100 metres of exposed lawn

▶ is time poor and leads a busy life

▶ wants to enjoy their garden on the weekend

▶ is house proud

▶ is prepared to pay extra for a professional service

▶ is aged between 30 and 60.

Competitor profile

There appear to be several lone gardeners and the major franchise gardening businesses offer services to the local area. A few live in the area, but others seem to service a wider area that includes Bulimba. They offer similar sorts of services. Some will only mow, while others offer landscaping and pool building. There does not seem to be a 'gardener' of choice in the local area who everyone turns too.

The Mulrenan brothers live locally and service the local business. They will offer a committed personalised service to their customers. They feel that this will help them connect with the community and stand apart from the competitors. Utilising photos they hope to build a community via social media and newsletters.

Legal, regulation, licence and insurance requirements for the business

The business will monitor any developments that may affect the garden practices they use and how they work with the environment. They will subscribe to gardening magazines, which normally alert them to any relevant issues.

Insurances

To mitigate risk the business will invest in the following insurances:

▶ public liability insurance

▶ asset insurance covering fire, theft and flooding

▶ professional indemnity

▶ workers' compensation.

Licences, permits, registrations and certificates

The business will obtain the following:

▶ advertising sign licence — Brisbane

▶ driver's licences

▶ vehicle registration

▶ commercial operator licence

▶ commercial wildlife licence

▶ permanent watering system licence

▶ wildlife harvesting licence (protected plants)

▶ WorkCover.

Sustainability

Mulrenan Gardeners will continually monitor best practice sustainable gardening practices. They will engage in earth-friendly practices and share the knowledge with the community via their blog, newspaper articles and workshops.

Mulrenan Gardeners will recycle where possible.

The business will be carbon neutral and carbon offsets will be purchased when necessary.

Business colours

Colour	CMYK (cyan, magenta, yellow, black)	RGB (red, green, blue)	Hex (hexadecimal)
Steel teal	C 0.3170 M 0.0070 Y 0.0000 K 0.4550	95,138,139	5F8A8B
Teal	C 1.0000 M 0.0000 Y 0.1650 K 0.5730	0,109,91	006D5B

Business logo

The Mulrenan Gardeners logo will be a green tree frog, which is the symbol of a happy environment. With permission, they intend to place the frog in a street-visible area for the houses that they service. To engage the community, they will run a competition inviting local senior schools to design their logo.

Customer relationship management

To encourage repeat business, customers will be offered a discount if they sign up to regular services, which they will be automatically billed for.

A monthly newsletter will be emailed to all clients or people who have inquired about services with the company. The content of the newsletter will also be pitched to the local paper.

Mulrenan Gardeners will sign up to the social media sites Instagram, Twitter, Facebook and Pinterest as they are ideal for showcasing photos. All the accounts will be linked and a filtered Instagram photo will be sent once a day, to build up a community around their business.

The business will be promoted to Andrew Mulrenan's past landscaping clients, and a commission will be paid to the landscaping business for clients who sign up to a regular service.

Seasonal fluctuations

	Spring	Summer	Autumn	Winter
Date	Sep–Nov	Dec–Feb	Mar–May	Jun–Aug
Temperature	14°C–28°C	20°C–30°C	14°C–29°C	11°C–23°C
Humidity	Medium – High	Highest	Medium	Lowest
Rainfall	Medium	Highest	Medium	Lowest

As the business is a gardening business it will be affected by the seasons. Grass grows faster with rain; however, mowing is difficult after extensive rain. So gardening schedules during the summer months may need to be flexible. Low rainfall will lead to less growth, and therefore the requirements for services are likely to reduce.

The business also needs to be aware of seasonal fluctuations with respect to the treatment, fertilisation and mulching of gardens.

Business equipment

Equipment to be bought outright:

▶ protective clothing $350

▶ two lawn mowers $700 each

▶ hedge trimmer $120

▶ hand-held leaf blower $100

▶ whipper snipper $120

▶ two wheelbarrows $90

Total: $2270

Equipment to be leased:

▶ green Holden ute with tray

▶ a computer for each brother

Total: $22 900 (40 monthly instalments + interest at 18%: 572.5 + 103.05)

Software solutions

Mulrenan Gardeners will use Google Apps for its business. It is free for the first ten users and will provide them with various cloud-based software tools including email, calendar documents and spreadsheets. The business will subscribe to XERO, an online accounting solution, which will cost $49 a month. The business will subscribe to OneSAAS (at $20 per month), which will enable it to automatically connect XERO to MailChimp, the newsletter service it plans to use.

Start-up financing

The start-up funds required are $2270, and the ongoing motor vehicle lease commitments are $675.55. The brothers will each invest $5000 of their own personal funds into the business and they will continue part-time work in their corporate roles while the business starts up, which will cover their personal funds.

The business will open a bank account with a debit card and will explore the cost of a portable merchant facility.

GST registration

The business is registered for the Goods and Services Tax as many purchases will be made through the life of the business. Initially managing of the financial accounts will be processed internally by Bruce's wife Sharron. As the business is in its early stages she will not be paid for this. Mulrenan Gardeners will engage a BAS agent to assist in processing the quarterly BAS statements and a local tax agent will be used to process the end-of-financial-year's accounts and to provide ongoing tax advice.

Intellectual property

The business is a simple gardening business and will not have intellectual property that needs protecting. All staff will be asked to sign a non-disclosure and non-competitive agreement to ensure they do not try to poach Mulrenan Gardeners' clients if they leave the business. The business name has not been trademarked but this is something that the business will consider doing, cash flow permitting.

Business recovery plan

The business will ensure all relevant insurances, inclusive of flood coverage, are in place to protect the business. Administration data will be maintained and backed-up in the cloud avoiding any issues that could occur with office and PC-based storage. A cloud-based wiki will be maintained to record business processes.

In the event of damage in the office, business processes and administrative data can be recovered in the clouds. Insurance will cover fire, theft, flooding and public liability.

Monthly budget profit and loss

Monthly Profit & Loss Budget for Mulrenan Gardeners

	Price	Jul-12	Aug-12	Sep-12	Oct-12	Nov-12	Dec-12	Jan-13	Feb-13	Mar-13	Apr-13	May-13	Jun-13	TOTAL	% of Total Income
No of Gardens		15	19	19	24	30	38	52	66	82	102	128	160	736	
Monthly Subscription			4	4	4	5	5	6	9	10	11	13	14	82	
Total Gardens		15	19	23	29	35	43	58	75	92	114	141	174	818	
Income															
Mowing	$50.00	750	938	972	1215	1519	1898	2623	3278	4098	5123	6403	8004	36820	
Gardening	$60.00	900	1125	1166	1458	1822	2278	3147	3934	4918	6147	7684	9605	44184	
Fertilising	$30.00	450	563	583	729	911	1139	1574	1967	2459	3074	3842	4802	22092	
Mulching	$15.00	225	281	292	364	456	569	787	984	1229	1537	1921	2401	11046	
Weed-Control	$15.00	225	281	292	364	456	569	787	984	1229	1537	1921	2401	11046	
Monthly Subscriptions	$85.00	1275	1594	1652	2065	2582	3227	4459	5573	6967	8708	10885	13607	62594	
Commission		0	0	0	40	0	0	0	120	0	0	60	0	220	
Total Income		3825	4781	4957	6196	7745	9681	13376	16720	20900	26125	32656	40820	187781	
Less Cost Of Sales															
Petrol	$8.00	120	150	188	230	282	346	466	600	739	911	1125	1391	6548	3.49%
Fertiliser	$4.00	60	75	94	115	141	173	233	300	369	456	563	696	3274	1.74%
Wages - Gardeners	$25.00	375	469	586	717	880	1082	1458	1875	2309	2847	3516	4348	20462	10.90%
Wages - Superannuation	$2.25	34	42	53	65	79	97	131	169	208	256	316	391	1842	0.98%
Wages - Training & Events		60	60	60	60	60	60	60	60	60	60	60	60	720	0.38%
Total Cost Of Sales		649	796	980	1186	1442	1759	2349	3004	3685	4530	5580	6886	32845	17.49%
															0.00%
GROSS PROFIT		3176	3985	3977	5009	6303	7922	11027	13716	17215	21595	27076	33935	154937	82.51%
Less Operating Expenses															
PEOPLE															
Admin - Wages & Salaries		0	0	0	0	0	0	300	300	300	300	300	300	1800	0.96%
Admin - Super Voluntary Contribution		0	0	0	0	0	0	0	0	0	0	0	0	0	0.00%
Admin - Training & Events		0	0	150	0	0	0	0	0	0	0	0	0	150	0.08%
Total PEOPLE		0	0	150	0	0	0	300	300	300	300	300	300	1950	1.04%

(continued)

Monthly budget profit and loss (*cont'd*)

Monthly Profit & Loss Budget for Mulrenan Gardeners (cont'd)	Jul-12	Aug-12	Sep-12	Oct-12	Nov-12	Dec-12	Jan-13	Feb-13	Mar-13	Apr-13	May-13	Jun-13	TOTAL	% of Total Income
PROMOTION														
Advertising	75	75	75	75	75	75	75	75	75	75	75	75	900	0.48%
Total PROMOTION	**75**	**75**	**75**	**75**	**75**	**75**	**75**	**75**	**75**	**75**	**75**	**75**	**900**	**0.48%**
PROVISION														
Bank Charges	12	12	12	12	12	12	12	12	12	12	12	12	144	0.08%
Accounting subscription	49	49	49	49	49	49	49	49	49	49	49	49	588	0.31%
Insurance	125	125	125	125	125	125	125	125	125	125	125	125	1500	0.80%
Maintenance	30	30	30	30	30	30	30	30	30	30	30	30	360	0.19%
Newspapers, Magazines	12	12	12	12	12	12	12	12	12	12	12	12	144	0.08%
MV - Lease Interest	103	103	103	103	103	103	103	103	103	103	103	103	1236	0.66%
MV - Petrol	70	70	70	70	70	70	70	70	70	70	70	70	845	0.45%
MV Rego + Insurance	18	18	18	18	18	18	18	18	18	18	18	18	216	0.12%
MV Maintenance	35	35	35	35	35	35	35	35	35	35	35	35	420	0.22%
Postage	12	12	12	12	12	12	12	12	12	12	12	12	144	0.08%
Stationery Supplies	15	15	15	15	15	15	15	15	15	15	15	15	180	0.10%
Telephone & Faxes	45	45	45	45	45	45	45	45	45	45	45	45	540	0.29%
Travel & Meal Allowance	15	15	15	15	15	15	15	15	15	15	15	15	180	0.10%
Travel & Taxis	15	15	15	15	15	15	15	15	15	15	15	15	180	0.10%
Total PROVISION	**556**	**556**	**556**	**556**	**556**	**556**	**556**	**556**	**556**	**556**	**556**	**556**	**6677**	**3.56%**
Total Operating Expenses	**631**	**631**	**781**	**631**	**631**	**631**	**931**	**931**	**931**	**931**	**931**	**931**	**9527**	**5.07%**
OPERATING PROFIT	**2545**	**3354**	**3195**	**4378**	**5671**	**7290**	**10096**	**12784**	**16284**	**20664**	**26145**	**33003**	**145410**	**77.44%**
Non-operating Expenses														
Electricity	0	0	120	0	0	0	0	120	0	0	0	0	240	0.13%
Home Office Supplies	0	12	117	0	12	0	12	117	0	12	0	12	295	0.16%
Total Non-operating Expenses	**0**	**12**	**238**	**0**	**12**	**0**	**12**	**238**	**0**	**12**	**0**	**12**	**535**	**0.29%**
													0	**0.00%**
NET PROFIT	**2545**	**3342**	**2957**	**4378**	**5659**	**7290**	**10084**	**12547**	**16284**	**20652**	**26145**	**32991**	**144874**	**77.15%**

Appendix C

Resources

Day 1: Are you ready to start a business?

- ▶ Springwise: www.springwise.com

- ▶ Australian Bureau of Statistics: www.abs.gov.au

- ▶ Survey Monkey: www.surveymonkey.com

- ▶ Etsy: www.etsy.com

- ▶ MadeIt: www.madeit.com.au

- ▶ NEIS New Enterprise Incentive Scheme: www.deewr.gov .au/Employment/JSA/EmploymentServices/Pages/NEIS.aspx

- ▶ Business Enterprise Centre (BEC): www.becaustralia.org.au

Day 2: Establishing your business

- ▶ Business.gov.au www.business.gov.au

- ▶ Carbonite: www.carbonite.com.au

- ▶ Dropbox: www.dropbox.com

- ▶ Evernote: www.evernote.com

- ▶ Government Forms: www.govforms.business.gov.au

- ▶ Queensland Government Smart Licences:
  www.sd.qld.gov.au/dsdweb/htdocs/slol

- ▶ Knowem?: www.knowem.com or
  NameChk: www.namechk.com

- ▶ The Grants & Assistance Finder:
  www.business.gov.au/Grantfinder/Grantfinder.aspx

- ▶ Australian Business Register: www.abr.business.gov.au

- ▶ Online business name generator:
  www.wordlab.com/gen/business-name-generator.php or
  Rhymer® by WriteExpress: www.rhymer.com/naming.html
  or Dot-o-mator: www.dotomator.com

- ▶ Visual Thesaurus: www.visualthesaurus.com

- ▶ IP Australia: www.ipaustralia.gov.au

- ▶ State government offices for licences, permits,
  registrations and certificates:

  - ✧ ACT   Canberra Connect
    www.canberraconnect.act.gov.au

  - ✧ NSW   NSW Government Licensing Services
    www.licence.nsw.gov.au/FAQ.htm

  - ✧ NT   Northern Territory Government
    www.nt.gov.au

  - ✧ Qld   *Smart*Licence
    www.sd.qld.gov.au/dsdweb/htdocs/slol

  - ✧ SA   Consumer and Business Service
    www.ocba.sa.gov.au

✧ Tas.   Service Tasmania Online
         www.service.tas.gov.au

✧ Vic.   Business Licences Victoria
         www.business.vic.gov.au

✧ WA   Department of Commerce
         www.commerce.wa.gov.au/index.htm

Day 3: Getting professional advice

▶ The International Coach Federation Australasia:
   www.icfaustralasia.com

▶ IP Australia: www.ipaustralia.gov.au

▶ Professional Bookkeepers: www.icb.org.au

▶ ACCA: www.australia.accaglobal.com

▶ CPA: www.cpaaustralia.com.au

▶ Chartered Accountants: www.charteredaccountants.com.au

Day 4: Marketing

▶ Colour palette generator:
   www.colorschemer.com/online.html

▶ Photobucket: www.photobucket.com

▶ Shorten and share hyperlinks: www.bitly.com

▶ Shorten and share hyperlinks and customise the URL:
   www.tiny.cc

Day 5: Finances

▶ Microsoft BizSpark:
   www.microsoft.com/bizspark/default.aspx

▶ AngelCube: www.angelcube.com

- ▶ Startmate: www.startmate.com.au
- ▶ Indiegogo: www.indiegogo.com
- ▶ Small business benchmarks: www.ato.gov.au/businessbenchmarks
- ▶ Australian Taxation Office: www.ato.gov.au
- ▶ Crowdfunding: www.indiegogo.com
- ▶ Pozible: www.pozible.com
- ▶ Kickstarter: www.kickstarter.com
- ▶ MYOB: www.myob.com.au
- ▶ XERO: www.xero.com

Day 6: People power

- ▶ OrgPlus: www.getorgplus.com.au
- ▶ Australia Job Search: www.jobsearch.gov.au
- ▶ Record keeping: www.business.qld.gov.au/business/ starting/starting-a-business/record-keeping-business/basic- record-keeping-requirements
- ▶ Privacy: www.privacy.gov.au
- ▶ Fair Work Infoline 13 13 94: www.fairwork.gov.au
- ▶ Tax File Number Declaration Form: www.ato.gov.au/content/6360.htm
- ▶ The Superannuation Choice form: www.ato.gov.au/content/downloads/SPR56761NAT13080.pdf
- ▶ Superannuation Clearing House: www.medicareaustralia.gov.au/super/index.jsp
- ▶ Occupational health and welfare: www.australia.gov.au/ topics/health-and-safety/occupational-health-and-safety

- ► Odesk: www.odesk.com

- ► Elance: www.elance.com

- ► Australian based site 'Freelancer': www.freelancer.com.au

- ► Australian Human Resources Institute: www.ahri.com.au

- ► State government WorkCover offices:

    - ✧ www.workcover.nsw.gov.au

    - ✧ www.workcover.vic.gov.au

    - ✧ www.workcoverqld.com.au

    - ✧ www.worksafe.act.gov.au

    - ✧ www.workcover.tas.gov.au

    - ✧ www.workcover.wa.gov.au

    - ✧ www.worksafe.nt.gov.au

Day 7: Launching your business

- ► Innovation Centre Sunshine Coast: www.innovation-centre.com.au

- ► River City Labs: www.rivercitylabs.net

- ► Fishburners: www.fishburners.org

- ► Founder Institute: www.fi.co/apply/sydney?secret=preview

- ► PushStart: www.pushstart.com.au

- ► StartPad : www.iaccelerate.com.au/startpad.html

- ► Startup Weekend: www.startupweekend.org

- ► York Butter Factory: www.yorkbutterfactory.com

- ► utbox: www.utbox.net

- ► Wikipedia: www.wikipedia.org

▶ Twiki: www.twiki.org

▶ Australia Post:
www.auspost.com.au/about-us/vision-mission.html to see
examples of vision and mission statements

▶ Trello project management tool: www.trello.com

▶ ToDoList: www.abstractspoon.com

▶ Australian Government business resource website:
www.business.gov.au/businessplan

Additional useful resources

▶ Small Business Support Line: 1800 777 275

▶ Business Enterprise Centre (BEC): www.becaustralia.org.au

▶ Flying Solo: www.flyingsolo.com.au

▶ Valerie Khoo: www.valeriekhoo.com

▶ International Coach Federation Australasian Region:
www.icfaustralasia.com

▶ Dynamic Business: www.dynamicbusiness.com

▶ My Business: www.mybusiness.com.au

Appendix D

Glossary

application programming interface (API) An interface between software programs that enables them to communicate. It unlocks the data from one software program enabling it to be mapped and flow into another software program.

best practice A method that consistently produces superior results in relation to other methods. As improvements are realised, the best practice method evolves and adopts the improvements.

billboard advertising Outdoor posters or signs that you see on streets and the highway.

customer relationship management (CRM) A system for managing an organisation's sales, marketing and support interactions with customers and clients. The purpose is to understand and deliver to the existing client base, thus maximising ROI and minimising expenses.

dadpreneur An entrepreneur who is a dad. Typically they may work part-time and run a home-based business around their children.

digital space   The computer technology space.

domain name   Unique website address location comprising of a combination of letters, numbers and hyphens.

due diligence   That you have properly checked and are aware of what is involved prior to getting involved in something.

e-commerce (electronic commerce)   The purchasing and selling of services and goods on the internet.

forum   An online message board where people can discuss ideas related to a particular topic.

franchise   A business structure whereby the franchisor develops a business model that is replicated and operated by franchisees, in exchange for a fee. Well-known franchise models include McDonald's and Boost Juice

GoToAssist   A service offered by Citrix Online that gives a user permission to connect with, access and drive another user's computer.

greypreneur   An entrepreneur who starts a business once they have retired from employment. They may run the business around their bowls commitments!

hosted   When a website is stored on a platform that enables users to access it over the internet.

incubator   An environment designed to nurture entrepreneurial start-ups through mentoring, resources and support.

intellectual property (IP)   An innovation or creation that can be owned and protected from other entities using it.

'in the clouds'   The clouds is a colloquialism for the internet.

micromanagement   A management style that involves closely controlling and monitoring the work of others.

Mind Your Own Business (MYOB) PC and online accounting software (buy the book *Learn MYOB in 7 Days* for more information).

mumpreneur An entrepreneur who is a mum. Typically they may work part-time and run a home-based business around their children.

New Enterprise Incentive Scheme (NEIS) A government-funded program for eligible job seekers who are interested in starting and running a small business. Visit www.deewr.gov.au/Employment/JSA/EmploymentServices/Pages/NEIS.aspx.

open source A methodology that involves the collaborative development of a product which is then shared for free. The product could be anything from a recipe through to software.

ordinary times earnings The ordinary hours of work, without any overtime.

Return on Engagement (ROE) Similar to ROI, rather than measure the return on money, the return on time invested is measured.

Return on Investment (ROI) A measurement used to evaluate the effectiveness and efficiency of the performance of an investment. It can be applied to a single investment or it can be used to compare investments. The calculation is:
(gain from investment − cost of investment) / cost of investment.

seed funding/financing The initial small investment at the start of a business cycle. The money may be used to pay for the development of a business plan.

SMART goal A set objective that you wish to achieve. A SMART goal is broken down to meet the following five criteria: Specific, Measurable, Attainable, Realistic/Relevant and Timely.

Software as a Service (SaaS) (pronounced 'sas') A form of on-demand software that is delivered over the internet and accessed by the user via a web browser. Rather than owning the software, you rent it. An example of SaaS is Google Apps.

solopreneur An entrepreneur who runs their own small business without employees.

trademark A term used to indicate the owner has legally protected their intellectual property. Users would need permission and to acknowledge they are using trademarked property. Misuse of trademarked property could result in fines being imposed.

tweet A microblog sent from the social media tool Twitter.

uniform resource locator (URL) A protocol for specifying the address of a website or a file located on the internet. An example is http://www.google.com.au.

vanity ID The popular, colloquial or personalised name of something. Typically it is easy to remember, but it may not be the real name. For instance, in New York there is a hotel called 'The Waldorf Hotel', but its real name is 'The Waldorf Astoria New York'.

VoIP (Voice over Internet Protocol) A technology that enables telephone calls to be made over the internet. Typically it is considerably cheaper than normal telephones. A well-known example of VoIP is Skype.

web domain *See* domain name

wiki A digital site that allows those with access to edit its content. It may be hosted internally or on a website.

wordmark   A type of graphical logo that is only text based. A well-known example is the Coca-Cola logo.

Xero   An online accounting software solution that you can access wherever you can access the internet. It features payroll, invoicing, billing banking and has a published API. With permission XERO can connect with some banks so transactions automatically feed into the solution.

Index

Invest in your business. Book Heather Smith today!

Heather Smith: Small Business Consultation

I help micro and small business owners implement systems that generate timely and accurate financial reports.

How? By finding out how something works, learning how it can assist in growing a productive and profitable business and then empowering businesses with this knowledge.

Working with XERO and MYOB, I help businesses determine the optimal solution for them and then train and support them.

Heather Smith: Speaker

My practical and informative presentations, delivered with warmth and wit, will engage, educate and entertain your audience.

Through consulting, training and interviewing small business owners (not to mention running my own small business) I know a lot about the inner workings of the small business world.

In particular, my talks about starting and growing a small business are full of useful stories and practical tips.

I am available for:

- ▶ keynote presentations
- ▶ group or workshop training
- ▶ installation and set-ups
- ▶ one-on-one consultation or training
- ▶ on-site and remote consultation
- ▶ fix-ups and forensic reviews of your data
- ▶ freelance writing for your small business magazine or blog.

You can find me on:

My website: www.HeatherSmithSmallBusiness.com

LinkedIn: www.linkedin.com/in/HeatherSmithAU

Twitter: @HeatherSmithAU

And don't forget to sign up for my free newsletter:
http://bit.ly/SignUp4Newsletter

Are you a member of an industry association or organisation? How about a sporting, not-for-profit or franchisee group? Then why not suggest booking me for your next conference or training workshop?

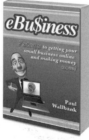